A
QUESTION
OF REALITY

A QUESTION OF REALITY

Kazimierz Brandys

Translated from the French by Isabel Barzun

CHARLES SCRIBNER'S SONS
New York

Library of Congress Cataloging in Publication Data

Brandys, Kazimierz.
A question of reality.
Translation of Nierzeczywistość.
I. Title.
PZ4.B82Qe [PG7158.B63]   891.8'537   80-10793
ISBN 0-684-16599-6

1 3 5 7 9 11 13 15 17 19   F/C   20 18 16 14 12 10 8 6 4 2

A
QUESTION
OF REALITY

Chapter 1

I SHALL NOT be speaking systematically. The list of questions which you are asking me to consider is long and detailed. I should prefer to regard it as an outline rather than to stick to it strictly. We did not discuss this during our conversation; it was not until the next day that I looked through the questionnaire. It would be rather ridiculous, you must admit, if I were to define my relation to God in answer to question twelve, then, at number thirteen explain my idea of marriage, and so on through the list. In explaining one's conception of marriage, one in fact defines to a certain extent one's relation to God, and vice versa. Human concerns overlap one another and it is difficult to deal with them one by one. So I shan't, as I say, answer you in a systematic manner. I think I understand what you're expecting of me, but I, too, expect something of myself. As you could see, I hesitated before agreeing to do what you proposed and I think anyone in my position would have reacted in the same way. In my case, though, considerations of safety were not my greatest concern. During our conversation, I noticed how you strove to dispel my fears. You emphasized the anonymous character of the tape recording and you told me several times that you would keep in mind the problem of my return home. I thank you for it. I do not doubt your good faith. I

1

know that for you my statements have only a sociological value. Your reputation as a scholar is sufficient guarantee for me. You will remember I mentioned in our conversation that I have no fears of the possible consequences.

I attach greater importance to the fact that you were born in Poland. I don't imagine I shall meet many American university professors who graduated from school in Warsaw the same year as I did. If I happen to mention the Four-Year Diet or *The Wedding* you won't have to refer to encyclopedias and textbooks. The Poles have a local complex. They know they speak in a code language that foreigners have no interest in deciphering. In our case, this will be one less hurdle to overcome. Very well, then. I plan to speak for half an hour every day, late in the evening, after my hotel has quieted down. I don't think I shall have any technical problems. The tape recorder works perfectly.

I could begin by answering the following question: *Do you feel that you are different from the people who come from non-Communist countries?* A parenthesis below contains a few subsidiary points. I am asked, for example, to specify whether what "differentiates" me from you is due to psychology, ethics, or habits. That's a very interesting question. I asked myself the same thing during our conversation, before I even knew what was in the questionnaire. And isn't it the very question that lies at the root of my resistance toward you, or rather my resistance to the suggestion you made to me—you remember—during our walk on the Nymveg Rijde, even before you finished telling me your plan? When I say that I *asked* myself this question I am not expressing myself accurately; I *felt* it. I was filled with misgivings, as if I were bound, at any moment, to make an inadvertent move that would betray me. When one goes to the doctor, one

2

generally has to answer a few preliminary questions concerning one's way of life, state of mind, sleeping habits, and the nature of the ailment. The patient tries to reply to the best of his ability, supplying as much detail as possible. He believes that his account is of the utmost importance to the doctor. Meanwhile, the doctor listens only perfunctorily but he is making mental notes: complexion, sallow; whites of the eyes, cloudy; nervous twitch of the foot. When it comes to making a diagnosis, those symptoms, unknown to the patient, are often more important than the ones he is aware of. In the same way, you will assess all my remarks as a set of symptoms, independently of what I have to say. Everything I may say will reveal a certain state of affairs I am not conscious of but which I shall betray and indeed confirm through the very things I have left unsaid; as well as through my way of dealing with a given problem or returning to it several times. Of course my monologue will be taken into consideration, but, even so, that does not mean that the authors of the questionnaires will be willing, for example, to match it with their own opinions, and to ask themselves whether mine do not make better sense. Each one of my remarks shall be seen in the light of reality from which they proceed, and will be analyzed together with my subconscious symptoms. This method is the standard as soon as one attempts a piece of applied scientific sociology, and yet it meets with resistance in me. I think this is a more or less normal reaction. After all, what each of us means to himself is his own most intimate experience. When our innermost experiences are used as a point of reference for the study of a much broader phenomenon, one of general interest, we feel debased in some way. That's the way we are made. One is always an exception for oneself, although questionnaires and statistics maintain the opposite. You and I feel, I suspect, the uniqueness of our existences, although we know how many millions of men live alongside of us, and how many millions of years have elapsed before us. Yet basically one needn't be ashamed of feeling this way about oneself. Of course, it is irrational, it embodies a salutary, lonely, indispensable illusion, without which individuality itself ceases to exist. I shudder to think what would become of us if we did not feel that we differed, each one of us, from the "average."

To this argument, your retort could be that questionnaires, tests, statistics form the very science of new social investigation. To me, they seem at times more like the new science of slavery. In sociology journals, you learn that five million people have the same salary, the same needs, the same ideas, and the same dreams as you have. Thereafter a seven-figure number serves as your consciousness; it is a number that takes the place of your personality. In the end, what is fashion if not a row of zeroes added on to someone's taste, and what is totalitarianism if not a row of zeroes added to someone's power? No doubt I am only one among many. Every era has people like me and every time they make up its anonymous substance. They are called the masses, the nation, society. Their lives are referred to impersonally as if they belonged to the times, and to the times alone. Yet as long as they live, they retain the illusion of their own individuality, and they survive precisely because of this monotheistic imprint that they carry within themselves. They hold their own against the numbers, against the atheist god of emptiness. That was the basis of my initial resistance.

You were invited here for a series of lectures at the university. I have come to attend an international conference on the theater. I also have to start rehearsals at "Studio XX." By chance we met in a city on the North Sea, and here we are conversing in Polish. Apropos of that, I noticed that you paid particular attention to my speech. From the outset you were interested in my vocabulary, my train of thought, and my mannerisms. You analyzed my syntax with great interest. Obviously, during the thirty-five years that you've been away from Poland, the language has changed. We speak a little differently. You used a few words which I had practically forgotten existed, even though they are completely correct, such as, for example, "albeit" and "it gravels me." These expressions are rarely used in Poland today; they have an old-fashioned flavor. On the other hand, you several times used the verb "implicate," which you undoubtedly borrowed from the modern English vocabulary. But that is not the point. As we listened to each other talk, we were sizing each other up. As we both know, language allows more than just a person's individuality to show through. If we talk about food, we always express a certain collective reality which has determined what we feel about food. The same applies if we talk about women or politics. Now it seems to me that I was completely unbiased as I listened to you, while you were listening to me with an already settled and specific goal: the study of the collectivity that was speaking through me. You listened to *how* I spoke. You wanted to ascertain whether my speech didn't perhaps disclose ready-made ideas already familiar to you, thought-clichés, a certain phraseological automatism, in short, the current symptoms of brainwashing. While I was talking, you were observing a man who has lived more than a quarter of a century in a country governed by Communists. Such a man, you thought, must surely be different, probably without being

5

aware of it. On this point I should like to make a slight correction. In my country, in present-day Poland, it can still happen that one is aware that certain things exist of which one is unaware! To come back to *the* question, I will say that, in a way, I accept the hypothesis that I am different from the people who live in your world, and that this may be a difference which it is impossible for me to be aware of. But at the same time, I think I am justified in putting forward hypothesis number two, which says that you may be equally incapable of understanding certain of the differences between you and the inhabitants of my world. Please note: I haven't the slightest doubt that you yourself believe in the reality of these differences. In that test, at least, we start out even.

You must be getting worried about the fact that I am going round and round the matter of my reservations about making this recording. Instead of *talking*, I am explaining why it is difficult for me to talk. Instead of talking about myself, I am talking about you. But I do remember that you asked me to talk about myself: above all, about myself. You advised me to stick to my own inner experiences, and not to make myself the representative of a majority, or a stereotype of some kind, not to project my personal experiences onto the problems of the age, and also to avoid coming to conclusions. Don't try to generalize, those were your very words, I think. Say "I" and not "Poland." Very well, but it will not be easy. A little while ago I mentioned the illusion of individuality. We have retained it, but it has been *in spite of everything*, not to say *against* everything. During the last half-century, several floors have been built on top of the sense we have of ourselves. I would call this phenomenon "a sort of inner urbanization of humanism." One can have one's own original viewpoints on numerous issues but,

6

for the last fifty years, dictatorships have replaced the consciousness of the individual with slogans for the masses, and the social sciences have more often worked with the concept of the "masses" and the "group" than with the "person." I have noticed more than once that I cannot think of myself as one. Any thought of this kind is arranged like the stories of a building, with numerous windows cut into it which open out upon different perspectives on space and time. When I think "I," at the very instant I think it, I place myself at the intersection of two axes: that of the relations among men, and that of the relations between man and time. One of the final points in your questionnaire is worded as follows: *Do you think that people of your country were happier a hundred years ago than they are now?* Not having lived at that time, I haven't the slightest idea what reply to make to the question. But one hundred, two hundred years ago, a person summing up his life would do it only with reference to his own life, that is, the period between his birth and his death. He would do it in relation to several dozen or several hundred people, and the only "floor" that was built above his own existence had to do with the life eternal. In those days, the human worlds were small and topped only by heaven. I, on the other hand, must in every one of my thoughts, view myself as injected into a universe of relations, transformations, and conditionings by which others have enlarged my consciousness. What I mean to say is that every effort has been made to ensure that each "self" should be rooted in its period, and that the period should be rooted in each "self." By the period, I mean the millions of men, events, and facts and all the tensions they cause; with all that there is of truth and falsehood, of the shameless, perverse, or deceitful in mankind; with, in fact, its capacity for cynicism, violence, and corruption; with

7

its indifference to justice and good sense; with, in addition, whatever there may be in it that is better or worse than what existed formerly or what may exist today elsewhere. You asked me to stick to my own subject. How can I? I sometimes have the impression that what I am dissipates itself in all directions, like a crowd in the streets of a city I might visit for the first time.

The questions that have to do with the biographical facts of my life bring me on to more solid ground. You have before you a person born on the eve of the First World War. My father was a professor before he became principal of a school. In 1933 I began to study law at the University of Warsaw, but two years later my parents learned to their surprise that I was studying philosophy. I did not devote more than two terms to it. In fact, my only real interest was art, and at the same time as I pursued my studies, I was taking jobs in the theater as an extra. In 1936, I dropped out of the university and enrolled in the National Institute of Theater Arts to study directing. Earlier it used to be The School of Dramatic Art. I should add that after graduating from high school, I did my military service as a cadet officer in the Signal Corps. From 1940 to 1944 I was a member of a group of Resistance fighters who joined the ranks of the organized Armia Krajowa, the AK. After 1945, I began to devote myself to directing plays (which I still do now, but less and less frequently). I am not a member of any political organization. During the years 1956 to 1968 I taught at the PWST in Warsaw, which is the present name of the school where I completed my studies before the war. Since 1970 I have been a "theaterologist" and I have a quiet little office at the National Institute of Fine Arts. I count on you not to confuse all these institutions, which have such similar initials.

I do not want to try your patience by telling you my

life story in detail, but if I am to go on answering questions about my point of view and my ethical principles, it seems inconceivable that I could manage to do so in a completely impersonal manner.

I mentioned my father's profession. That he was a teacher does not tell you a great deal; I must try roughly to define his mind and the influence he had on me. The father figure often has the weight of a prototype. The father is the first person, or at least the first man, with whom we have any dealings, to whom we compare ourselves, the first whom we judge. What is more, he is a mysterious silhouette in our lives, endowed with an extra dimension: the past. The child does not know what is meant by the future; life to him is one impatient curiosity, a sort of unreal state between "today" and "tomorrow." What happened before we were born, that which our legends and symbols will rest upon for a long time, all that is associated with the figure of the father. The phrase "when I was your age" that we hear throughout our childhood is our first contact with history. Our first Tacitus, our first Plutarch is the man who directed our sights toward the historic past tense.

My father handed down to me the nineteenth century. There were revolutions and uprisings, there was industrial growth, oppression, and emigration. I learned about all this under his roof, probably very young, and what resulted was a kind of iconographic story of his life. Although he was born toward the end of the last century, to me he was a rebel, an emigrant, a convict deported to Siberia, and a positivist. Such a picture of history incarnate is like a dream from which one gradually awakens as one grows up. Yet many people remain immersed in these childish dreams for their entire life. I would find it difficult to say exactly when I began to think

9

for myself. Perhaps it was not until the war. During the first months of the occupation, my father wore a railroad worker's cap. Why, I can no longer remember, but the first time that I saw him wearing it, I was struck dumb with astonishment and fright. There is no doubt this sight roused me from my childhood dreams forever. From that moment, my father became for me a contemporary figure. The cap had transformed him into a mere passerby.

In general, we know history only in its most innocent guise. It is only later that its demons come to torment us. When President Narutowicz was assassinated in Warsaw in 1922, I was eight years old. I was not able to understand the motives of the man who killed him. All I remember is that, on a cloudy day, my father came home, his boots covered with mud, and said, "They did it." There was, it seemed, a "they." It then occurred to me that genuine history was being kept hidden from me, just like certain books in our little library: I was not allowed to read them, I was not old enough. The sins of this world were being kept hidden from me: poverty, politics, prostitution and the mysteries of sex. It was the very principle of education. And, come to think of it, it was not so very stupid— anyhow not more stupid than the education given to Adam. Without forbidden fruit, there is no paradise, and the apple from the tree of knowledge ripens in order to be plucked.

All this may not be altogether clear; it is difficult for me to see myself as distinct from my small group of school friends. One does not acquire one's beliefs all alone but rather by getting to know one another under the Tree of Knowledge. Two years before graduating from school a few of us already held some beliefs. I do not intend to summarize them for you. These were ready-made well before we had the time to formulate them for ourselves.

10

They were waiting for us, just as the various branches of the military await recruits. One would plunge into socialism, another into nationalism. As for me, it was the heritage of democratic tolerance which fell to my lot. The spirit of understanding and moderation was waiting to take me to its bosom. I cannot say much more; all of it happened simply enough but in a manner somewhat vague.

What were the factors, what were the circumstances that influenced my view of the world? I have two views of the world: one in my periods of depression, the other when I enter a period of vitality. Apart from that, I may happen to have opinions about events and men—but I do not believe that these make up my view of the world. At best, I may ponder my relation to the world, but that is a somewhat different matter; I would almost say it is something closer to the view that the world has of me than the other way around. To be candid, certain points raised by the questionnaire do not correspond to anything in my experience. For example, as regards my university studies, it seems to be taken for granted that during those years, my mind became "enriched by a certain body of knowledge" within my chosen field. That presumption is false, to the very extent that my mind at that time was enriched in a much more concrete way by a completely different lesson! I refer to the concussion that I suffered when someone hit me on the head with a stick. That is an important episode in the history of my relationship with the world: it made me realize, in a forcible way, the view that the world itself held of my person. It prompted me to reflect much more deeply than my course on Roman law.

We used to take our examinations three or four students to a group. I was fairly well prepared and already had behind me the examinations on the theory of law,

11

the history of Polish institutions, and the history of procedure. I decided to take a breath of fresh air and went out into the courtyard with a friend. I had only one examination left to take: Roman law. We were walking outside the library when we heard behind us the sound of running followed by a shout. I turned around. A man on the ground was trying to shield his head with his hands. At the same time, a number of students wearing the cap of a right-wing youth corps passed by us. One of them, wearing boots, was carrying a stick. A moment later, when I was trying to rescue the man who was lying before me, I was stunned by a sharp pain at the base of the skull. I must have lost consciousness for a few seconds. I certainly don't remember going back inside the building on my own two feet. Nor do I remember which questions I answered on Roman law. I only know that after the last one I collapsed. When I was picked up, the professor told me, "You've passed, despite your having overworked." The next day I woke up in a hospital bed. I had a concussion, caused, as they say, by "a blow from a blunt instrument."

It was my first contact with physical terror. Moments of this kind are experienced in shame. I must have felt somewhat like a woman who has been raped: impotence and rage with an element of sordidness as well. And along with it was the Chaplinesque comedy of the situation, the savior falling beside the victim he seeks to rescue. All that was boiling up inside me: I had to let off steam at someone and my father served as a scapegoat. Reassured about my health and my examination results, he saw fit to close the incident with an old Polish saying: "You will get better long before you get married. . . ." I was thunderstruck. I regained the use of my tongue, knowing that every word was hurting him. I was finding in him a strange trait which irritated me although I could not define it exactly, a sort of shuffling honesty combined with something else . . . something perhaps akin to dissimulation or hypocrisy.

I still had not the slightest idea what the old school of silence is. Of course, my father was an honest man, to such a degree that his mind could never grasp the extent of human baseness. But I knew another side of him. He was sufficiently sensible to understand the significance of my misadventure at the university. The facts were horribly clear: I had helped a man to get up who had been beaten raw, I had come to his aid, and in return, I had got a nasty blow on the head. The vileness of that act had surely struck him, and yet, when I told him that in Polish universities "they" were massacring people for the sole reason that they were Jews, I felt that my words—implicating those same, base individuals—aroused an agitation of another kind in my father. As far as one could tell, he resented my calling by their proper names events which it was proper to hush up. And it was proper to hush them up for certain delicate reasons, socio-familial or patriotic reasons. My father would have preferred never to hear such words as "Jew," "blood," or "massacre." No doubt, because he was not anti-Semitic and did not like brute force, he considered any mention of anti-Semitism and physical violence as a vulgar want of tact. And yet he had to know what was going on in the universities. It occurred to me that to know the facts and to know the truth are not exactly the same thing, and I still had to learn that a man who does not know himself is incapable of knowing the truth. Our discussion took place at the table. While surreptitiously watching my father—he was busy dunking his croissant into his cup of coffee—I let drop a few comments on the way in which the Poles had adopted the tradition of the Russian pogroms, after which I asked him if he had taken as much pleasure eating his croissant

13

after the assassination of Narutowicz. At that point, my father stood up suddenly and slapped my face.

I have just listened to the tape from the beginning. Perhaps I should have stuck to the questions in sequence after all. It seems I am still speaking *beside* or *instead of* the point, and running the risk of falling into an autobiographical tale, bespangled with memories. The memories broadcast by the machine at the simple touch of a button sound like a confession blared through a megaphone. These last ones especially. Listening to myself talk, I seem to hear someone talking to me who is imitating my voice, someone who must have secretly witnessed my argument with my father. But what can I do about it? I will keep going. After all, I can destroy the tape, send you back the tape recorder, and send you a written excuse. Nevertheless, I am anxious to keep going, first, in order to find out whether I am capable of revealing myself without reserve; second, to see if I am capable of considering my life in a more or less rational and objective way; third, to try to learn something about myself that I do not already know. Enough for today; more tomorrow.

Chapter 2

THE SCENE with my father took place exactly as I have described it, but my comments on it date from today. At the time I was, at the very most, suspicious. Something had come between us; in his hemming and hawing fashion my father was honest, and I was unable to express honestly my own honesty. That may seem somewhat complicated but it is basically very simple. We were both honest people or—as my father would say—honest Poles: only I was a Pole who had suffered a concussion.

At the outset the blow had stunned me, but after I regained consciousness, I was to begin to see things differently, to see my own country, my true fatherland in action. No longer through literature or through history. Poland had caught me, tested me, and thrashed me. Lying on the ground I heard neither singing nor hymns, only turmoil and uproar. It was a shock, certainly, but at least it brought on a reaction. My rage and humiliation sought arguments. The very next day I was all set, on principle, to bash in the face of anyone in defense of my own cause. I had, therefore, reacted normally, like a free man, the way a Frenchman or an American would. The way one fights *with oneself*. At times like this my father would begin to hem and haw, because for him *with oneself* meant with one's own *people*. I suppose that he could not conceive of any servitude other than to his country. He felt himself to be free, since he lived in a Poland governed by Poles.

I remember one of Sienkiewicz' sayings which he inscribed in a friend's guest book in 1914, soon after I was born and two years before his death: "Beware of nations that prefer liberty to the fatherland . . ." Seven nations were just about to massacre each other obediently in the name of seven fatherlands. As for Sienkiewicz, he no doubt was thinking of Poland in the days of the nobles and the succession of partitions that we had to suffer. To tell the truth, the misfortunes of Poland cannot be explained by our excessive love of liberty. Rather, they can be attributed to the excessive love for itself felt by a fraction of the nation; and from what I know of the author I know what he meant. Nonetheless, the saying implies something extraordinary for us who, here and now, see how dictatorships have mastered the art of imposing on freedom "blackmail through the fatherland" (and vice versa). That was something that Sienkiewicz had not foreseen. Even so, he ought perhaps to have perceived the madness of such a choice as *either* the fatherland *or* liberty. Yes, but in order to see in this *"either/or"* the threat of a two-way blackmail, more than one Pole, even today, would have to get hit over the head with a stick on Krakowskie-Przedmiescie Avenue—wielded, what is more, by another Pole—as I did in my time. You wanted me to talk about myself. I am prepared to do so: the concussion awoke in me a lobe of consciousness which until that time had been half asleep. I became capable of thinking normally, just as one is able to breathe normally once more after having a pneumothorax.

In painting a picture of my father, I wanted to dwell upon a certain type of Pole, a strong and fruitful type, with descendants and a family tree. In Tolstoy's diary—

16

which I was reading just before I left—I found a little note made up of a single phrase: "The pure Russian type—pure through lack of contact with life." This was a Russian writer's comment about certain Russians of his time. This observation, accurate as it is, applies neither to my father nor to me, and yet it struck me.

Poles are not at all given to making statements of this kind. You must have noticed the calm tone of the remark; Tolstoy noted in passing a character trait which seemed to him to be a typical element of the psychology of certain Russians. With us, such a characteristic, if it does not remain completely unnoticed, is immediately elevated to the rank of eternal Polishness. It is as if the individual in Poland had no psychology of his own, as if there were only a national psychology. In speaking of my father I have just such a psychological type of Pole in mind. As I said, a Pole with a family tree and many offspring. No doubt he resembles Tolstoy's "Innocent Russian," cut off from reality. Perhaps Tolstoy saw certain traditions reflected in this character and certain consequences proceeding from him. Whatever it was, he drew the sketch from life. Such characters then entered into the realm of literature, and people recognized themselves there. So it was in England and in France.

One more thing: in Poland, literature also borrows its characters from life, but only within limits. There could be no question of analyzing psychology in its true human, or interhuman, complexity; an internal censorship was at work. One could not set the hero of a Polish novel off onto paths which might lead him to his downfall, or into madness or crime! The things that happened in the works of Balzac or Dostoyevsky—such as when a man robs another of his fortune or murders a woman for love—were not acceptable in *our* literature. In Polish books, the hero

17

represents the nation, and the plot arises out of the story of his love affair with the fatherland. With such constraints, it is impossible to present true passions, or to create complete human personalities. Impossible, because certain of the forces that motivate men must remain hidden, being the very ones which push men into the most significant and desperate situations. There is no chance to reveal the social, biological, and metaphysical components of life if they cannot be developed to the full in the life of the hero, if one must stop before the final consequences. One mustn't sink into madness, mustn't betray, mustn't kill, mustn't bring *dishonor* on oneself by one's *weaknesses*—how can one under such conditions avoid some feeble compromise, even if purely literary? Throw oneself under a train? Even then, the suicidal Pole would be hauled off the tracks by another Pole. What is left? A mysterious death. And yet, in this country as in others, murder, corruption, rape, selfishness, prostitution have all been rife. It has been a country inhabited by men and women with all their baseness, all their sins. There were romantics, dreamers, yes, but also shopkeepers, workingmen, and whores. In a Polish novel, the hero must be a romantic, and the manufacturer a patriot. And, for two hundred years, the only female character in Polish literature has been the ghost of a little dead girl . . .

The result: society has ceased to know itself. From time to time, but only infrequently, society's awareness of itself has been disclosed in lampoons. As you know, that also is part of our culture, which has long known how to make fun of itself. I said that Poland has suffered from a provincial complex made up of bitterness, pride, and a somewhat perverse elitism. It reminds one of certain families that have fallen on hard times and who ridicule their own ruin and past follies, but are unable to exist outside their own circle or to repeat their anecdotes anywhere else, because no one outside would be able to appreciate them. With the passing years this circle becomes completely sealed off. It then becomes impossible to distinguish what comes from necessity and what from choice. Finally one sees a few ghosts appear, but only the eccentrics to whom they speak are able to understand their mumblings. For they are the only ones who know that, in these admonitions and allusions, this muttering which is incomprehensible to the uninitiated, there is a note of truth. Truth which is no less true for not being understood by strangers—in general, one does not grasp the truths that one has not been able to experience. And once again, doubts arise: are these local truths or universal?

But let us return to our subject. In the things I said just now about the inhibitions of our literature, there is basically nothing new. Others said and wrote the same things seventy or even a hundred years ago. They occurred to me in connection with my father. All these limitations were deeply rooted in him—that special way of not talking about the portion of ugliness which truth brings with it, of refusing to sharply observe facts and men, a fear of reality. All this was held within the mold of the nation as if in a container which would explode if its contents were too hot or too cold. If my father had been a writer, he would have written just that sort of fiction. He could have been the author of all our *great* novels. I repeat: of just those, just as they are, stereotyped, and not of any of the others. He was born almost at the same time as they were, and of the older works, he remembered only the most comfortable parts, those least critical of the nation. I wonder if he even knew how to hate anything besides the image he had created of "the Russian" and "the Prussian." The day Narutowicz was assassinated, when he came home and exclaimed: "They did it," he seemed honestly overwhelmed. And yet, even then, he left something unsaid, he shied away from something. No doubt from the name of the "National" party.

During the first months of the occupation, I met an acquaintance in the street whom I had known before the war, an instructor at the YMCA sports club. After my misadventure at the university, I had taken up boxing. My instructor was named Rabczyn. He was a taciturn man, in control of himself. During training, he would bestow his advice in a calm voice; he was rarely seen to smile. It was our meeting in November 1940 that led me to take part in the Resistance. The group headed by Rabczyn had a military character—after the defeat of September 1939, I myself escaped from a column of prisoners, thereby avoiding a stay in the P.O.W. camp—and, as the group was a center for directing the armed struggle, I considered myself under his command. Later, my activity in the Resistance was to take on a quite startling aspect, even though, within the organization itself, my role was rather modest—I was a private second class. I will come back to that. The years we spent together permitted me to get to know Rabczyn well. When I spoke about my father just now, I described him as the fruitful type of Pole. Rabczyn was among the spiritual descendants of that kind of Pole; his character traits and his reactions often reminded me of my father. It is striking how the strength and persistence of those traits carry through generations and eras. Rabczyn's view of the world—I am not referring so much to his views as to his way of experiencing the world— was limited to the national scale; it ignored the two dimensions of the individual and of humanity. When I told him one day about my mother's illness—she had been operated on for cancer during the war—I sensed his surprise. "So that's how it is," he murmured after a moment. "It is the Poles who have suffered most. That's how it is. . . ." I was astounded. My mother's operation actually had nothing to do with the sufferings of the country; her illness had begun just before 1939! In this piece of illogic which I hadn't even the right to take notice of, I found something of a family likeness. Rabczyn was an honorable man. I admired his moral strength, his energy, and his courage. Yet he sometimes left me gasping. For this honest man, who was far from stupid, could see in the war and the persecutions, and the people's misery and misfortunes, only the national tragedy of Poland. If I began to talk to him about the sufferings of the Jews, the Russians, or the Dutch, he did not contradict me, but he stayed mute. Likewise, he would be silent, assuming a somewhat abstracted air, whenever in our conversations I would touch upon some fact bearing witness to the existence of human passions. Either he pretended not to know what hatred or vanity were, or he did not believe in their existence. To me, that savored of hypocrisy. But perhaps he thought that God and Man were Polish, after all. Perhaps he thought that everything divine and humane is thriving and healthy on Polish soil, while beyond stretches the unhealthy land of psychological and philosophical considerations.

I will not use the true names of the people that I mention, but that of Rabczyn is real. He died during the Warsaw Uprising. I sometimes wonder how his life would have continued, what he would do and think today if he had survived. He could of course have emigrated. It is hard to guess how he would have faced the circumstances which determined, after the war, the life of each of us. In 1945 or in 1950, he could have been arrested after a political denunciation, although he was never involved in

21

politics, neither during the occupation nor at any other time. It is very difficult to imagine what his fate would have been, and more generally, the fate of Poles of his type. And here am I, put in the position of having to reply to the seventh question in the questionnaire: *What is your attitude toward the idea of freedom?*

My attitude? It is mixed—characterized at once by humility and by complexity. Freedom certainly means something different to me from what it did to my father and those like him. Perhaps they felt freer than I do. They were less aware. Certainly less aware of themselves. They felt free in their thoughts and in their actions and were not conscious of the weight of the restrictions to which they, too, were subjected in those two areas: hereditary, almost genetic restrictions. These are usually accounted for by the past, by the handicap resulting from the successive occupations which the country had experienced. But that is too simple to be true. In truth, these inhibitions date from *before*. For, after all, the type of man for whom freedom means the right to individuality came into being in Europe through social conflicts and religious battles. In Poland, these men were stultified with slogans about class solidarity and later about national unity. Slogans which, as it turned out, were replaced by make-believe: the semblance of tolerance, of freedom, and later of solidarity. Make-believe, because freedom, tolerance, and national solidarity in Poland have never included the entire society. Whence, *the Polish unreality*. The type of Pole who does not know himself or the world, the good Pole, has perpetuated himself for generations, not to achieve his perfect form until after uprisings and partitions. I don't know if I make myself clear. But why have we not had a Shakespeare? Or a Molière, a Balzac, or a Gogol? . . . Undoubtedly because we have not experienced any great social movements or any centralized power. England had Shakespeare, Russia had Gogol because in those two societies the truths of life stood out in sharper relief than in Poland. Their histories were more unabashedly *loud*. And this is true despite all the differences that separate them. Despotic oppression, corruption, and poverty created a certain idea of fatality in Russia. And the king's bloody battle with Parliament, the bourgeoisie, the peasantry, and the Church shaped the historical and human dramas of England. I have an idea that Balzac would not have existed if a certain chain of events, vulgar and greedy, like guillotines and banks, had not preceded him. The situations in which man has to hate and fear, to desire certain possessions, to command and act in this or that direction, are engendered by strong social tensions. Brutal and dangerous situations they are, and ones which strip a man naked. It seems that only from such situations is culture born. All contemporary culture shows enormous scars of this kind—of political struggles, of the development of laws, of *interests* in the widest sense of the word. It is all one whether the interests are commercial, aristocratic, or plebeian. When all is said and done, it is not artists alone who create culture, but also sailors, engineers, and craftsmen. Yes, and philosophers. It is a pity that we are not able to distinguish within culture the part which is concrete, the empirical world, and the part which is spiritual. But we know for certain that the ideal side is inseparable from the material. It was in the factories that the Declaration of the Rights of Man was forged.

It may happen that one talks about these problems in Poland, too, but they are not part of our historical experience. They have never been engraved on the psyche of people like my father. Rarely did such people know about the business of banks, or how the stock market works, or the ways of the market. Likewise, they knew nothing of the inner workings of political struggle. They were not the children of the civilization but the sons of the nation. The lack of freedom distorts the picture of the world. In subject countries, life reveals its true contents not through an evolutionary process but only through upheavals and catastrophes. For two hundred years the greatest tensions of our past have been resolved in sudden and brutal jolts. Romanticism and positivism represented the two breakthroughs of imagination and insight, the twofold reflex which is the consequence of such violent collective experiences as uprisings. But the greatest experience of our society, that which brought into play the heaviest forces, was the Second World War. Never before had the human condition in Poland been so thoroughly exposed. That lesson could have taught us to know ourselves, and it should have transformed the relationship of the Polish people to the rest of the world; but its meaning and possibilities were quickly obliterated. Already, we have here the essence of our problem. Neither my father nor Rabczyn could have understood it. They both lived within the Polish unreality, as I have said, in the national myth, not on the true scale of the individual's relation to civilization. That is perhaps why they felt freer than I do. And yet it seems to me that for my part—despite a more acute awareness of the limitations put upon my freedom—I was in large measure freer than they.

I am using here certain words in an entirely personal way. I think, for example, that a man who dies for freedom may not necessarily be free in spirit. The refusal to fight is sometimes a greater proof of freedom than a heroic death. Indeed, I cannot doubt the moral strength which is necessary to become a rebel or to rise up in revolt. Certain acts, even if less well known, require more determination and courage than any act of heroism. I do not know if you have ever heard of the Polish uprising which broke out in Siberia in 1866. It was well organized and even had its own underground press. It was fomented by some Poles who had been deported to Siberia after the January 1831 uprising. The organization chose to call itself the Siberian Legion. The leader was a pianist from Warsaw who took command of seven hundred Polish convicts and turned them into a detachment of mounted troops. The Legion was defeated after a battle that took place near Lake Baïkal; its leaders were shot. Prince Kropotkin claims in one of his works that Russian convicts, as opposed to the Polish, used to submit passively to their fate. The editor of the Polish edition, in his notes, criticized the author for his injustice to the Russians; the revolt of the Russian convicts was also being planned, but it did not come to anything because they were betrayed by one of the conspirators. I would also make a point of the fact that after the battle of Baïkal the rules of the camp were made less stringent and the treatment of the Poles improved markedly.

I am keeping in mind the question concerning my idea of freedom. During our conversation, you asked me about the extent of political freedom in Poland. Among other things, you asked me a question which turned up again in the questionnaire: *In what ways does the national consciousness of your countrymen manifest itself?* As you must have noticed, I have skirted the issue. Poland is not the only place where such things are deliberately not mentioned. The nation, the fatherland, patriotism—these are words used often and willingly on television and in the press. But when I was sitting with you in that quiet "cellar" in Rubens Square, I realized that I would have to explain to you in detail certain circumstances, circumstances difficult for an outsider to understand and difficult to put into words, even for me. Today, the needs of the national consciousness in Poland are satisfied primarily through audiovisual means. Films are made on the Age of the Piasts, or the novels of Sienkiewicz are adapted to the screen. For three hours, the spectator can watch the Polish hero, with holy medals around his neck, defeating Tartars and Swedes with his holy sword. He feels secure in his *Polishness* and sustained by Polish tradition. When he leaves the movie theater he can read the papers' reviews that reinforce this feeling in him—reviews imbued with the flavor of "Old Poland," patriotically sentimental. As for reviews emphasizing that today there is no patriotism without an awareness of the rights of Man and that the freedom of the nation depends upon the respect paid to these rights, you will not find any in any organ of the press. The sons of workers, peasants, and intellectuals sitting in their cinema seats are fascinated by the image, in brilliant color, of a nobleman on horseback! Which is absolutely insane. Especially if one remembers where and when it is all taking place: in Poland, thirty years after the takeover by the reformers' party, which, in its politico-ideological statements, appealed at the outset to the Jacobin tradition and the glorious history of the Polish proletariat! In order to explain these mysteries, I would have to initiate you into further mysteries, and a great many of them. . . . I should have to explain to you how, and after what kinds of twists and turns, in a Poland governed by Communists, the defense of the Czestochowa monastery against the Swedes in 1655 was "brought to the screen" and has become a patriotic alibi for the holders of power. Let us say that these questions are somewhat too complicated for a foreigner. For myself, I see it as a kind of spiritism. The circumstances are new, the setting is different, society has been rebuilt, but the magic-lantern, make-believe mind of Poland is still there, in spite of several exorcisms and peregrinations—as if it obeyed the law of the vicious circle: everything back in its place.

And what frightens me the most is that today glorification of our Polish past has been made official, that for some reason it has become a necessity for some people, and that it has won approval from outside. Not only the sword and the medal, but also more recent military scenes, the September war, partisan helmets, pitched camps in the woods . . . and anti-Semitism. I have a fear that all this may soon become *Polish folklore*, and our proud nationalists will not realize it until it is too late, and they, and we, will be swallowed up, along with all the folklore. And our tradition of national resistance will be tolerated with good nature. For that may be part of the plan: somewhere there are gentlemen sitting at their desks who have known for a long time that they cannot help including in the package this one more little piece of nationalism for home use only. . . . Yes, at this thought I am truly terrified.

Question seven in your inquiry raises five related points. The first is: *Do you think that the idea of freedom finds its embodiment in the course of history through the evolution of society and the progress of civilization?*

Yes, of course. But not in a simple way. Let us define our terms. By the word *freedom* one can mean a juridico-political state, or a social utopia, or again a human aspiration. I myself believe that one gains one's own freedom by oneself, but that is an entirely personal opinion. Obviously, it is psychological and individual freedom that I mean. In that sense, one could wonder to what extent, if any, the American of today is freer than a citizen of the ancient republic of Rome. I have no pat answer, and I don't even think that there is an answer, merely some hypotheses or some mental constructs. But I'm aware that your question has something else in view.

If I get arrested for acts which the law does not forbid, if I am condemned by a court which is unable to resist the pressure of the government, I consider that my freedom has been infringed. Likewise if I found it impossible to get an article criticizing the government published in any newspaper. I am speaking here, of course, of the conditions governing external freedom, its legal and constitutional guarantees. To be sure, the abolition of slavery and the right of peasants to own property were enactments that enlarged the scope of freedom, embodying the idea of freedom, as the wording of the question puts it. One could choose to understand things in this way. But I repeat: not in a simple way. The paths of progress cross each other, the line of evolution often shows contradictions and paradoxes—do I need to persuade you of that?

Let us take the examples nearest to us. In Russia and in Poland, the peasants acquired the right to own property almost simultaneously. Among liberal circles at the court of Saint Petersburg, in the 1860s, serfdom was seen as a shocking anachronism. And we know that Alexander II personally hated the aristocracy. The need for enfranchisement could no longer be denied. The Czar's own brother led the partisans of reform, the promoters of the plan being a small group of highly cultivated liberals. The program was bold: the reforms were to free the peasants of legal bondage and give them land. It was a large-scale social measure in the making. Herzen, who had exiled himself to London, wrote about the Czar with great esteem—Alexander II was then seen as the liberator, the savior of Russia.

But the reform movement ran into resistance from the conservative elements who were in power: the generals and the landowners. Members of these circles forced the decree to be revised and postponed. In June 1862, several fires broke out in Russia. One of them, in Saint Petersburg itself, began near the government buildings. The Minister of the Interior only barely escaped from the flames. There turned out to be no fire engines; the authorities did nothing; the chief of police was not to be found. Then rumors began to spread, denouncing the Poles and the revolutionaries as the incendiaries. The liberal party lost influence, the originators of the radical reform project were pushed aside, and it was revised to accommodate the interests of the landowners. In exchange for their freedom, the peasants were to be burdened with ruinous payments for their land. The Czar had come to lean toward the side of the conservative opposition. The battle for postponement intensified; dire rumors circulated creating an atmosphere of provocation and conspiracy. Arrests followed. The final date set for the emancipation of the peasants was February 19, 1863. In Poland the uprising began on January 22. The immediate cause was the problem of compulsory military service in the Czar's forces. For the Russian army the battle against the partisans turned out arduous. The enormous expeditionary force was ordered to close ranks, while the rebels practiced the modern tactics of guerrilla warfare; they eluded capture incessantly. At that point they still enjoyed the support of a segment of the population. The rebel government proclaimed the redistribution of land, thus reawakening the hope of social measures in the heart

29

of the peasantry—many peasants began to pay taxes to the National Treasury. Long years later, the Russian officers would recall how poor the morale was among their troops: they would advance and retreat in the woods as if paralyzed; the threat of danger was constant. This gloomy war, without victories or outcome, seemed as if it would never end. Yet an outcome was reached from another quarter: Saint Petersburg. While the uprising was raging, two special envoys arrived in Poland; they were two of the originators of the first radical plan for emancipation who had in the meantime been kept in the distance: Milution and Tcherkarski. They had been sent on their mission by the Czar himself: go to Poland and put your red plan into practice. They fulfilled their mission within a few months. Traveling through the countryside, they distributed the land to the peasants. What the government had proclaimed, the envoys effected. The Polish peasant received his land from Russian hands. In the countryside, support for the partisans ceased. The uprising was checked.

Perhaps I have gone too fast, in which case I will ask you to go back a bit and listen to me again. The outline of those events is, in fact, widely known, though historians might have much more to say. What interests me personally is simply the plot and its development. I would go so far as to say, the way in which it was worked out. Do we not have here something like a tale composed with an astonishing command of narrative technique? Are we not seeing, as it were, the expression of a philosophical attitude toward life—not, I think, benevolent; perverse, rather? Perhaps. Purposes, causes, and effects, individual motives, and group interests, their inner workings and their machinery are revealed to us in all their diabolical intricacy and confusion: freedom as the result of provocation; freedom obtained at the price of freedom. Reactionary forces liberating progressive forces and vice versa. After the redistribution of land, the Polish peasants helped the occupying forces to lay hands on the rebels. In Russia, the abolition of serfdom brought on a wave of police retaliation that lasted several decades. In Poland, the peasant received land, but all hope of national autonomy immediately evaporated. In the country of the Czars, serfdom was abolished but the prisons were filled. Of course, I am schematizing. In life, such contrasts are not so obvious; day-to-day life conceals them and muffles them as with dirty cotton.

I wanted to give you a rough idea of the zigzag graph that one episode of social emancipation traced on the chart, one single reform. Let that be the answer to the seventh question in the survey, that is, to the first of the five related points.

A few more words, though I am not sure which to choose. I am trying to speak clearly, but I sometimes get the feeling that I fall into professorial clichés. That happens to me sometimes. For several years I was not able to do without the phrase "in a certain sense." I would use it at the beginning of one sentence out of three. When I realized what I was doing, I came to the conclusion that this linguistic habit reflected my awareness of the ambiguity of things. "In a certain sense," a thing can be right or useful. In another, it can be stupid or harmful. Life comprises many senses or meanings; each of them taken separately reveals a part of the truth; taken together, they suggest the idea of relativity. Modernity has infiltrated our language. Even my comments (and I am aware of this also) are a modern reflex. A symptom of excessive self-consciousness, of a self-diagnostic and self-critical culture. Of thinking about thinking. Never before, perhaps, have there been so many wise men alive at one time, and probably so many stupid ones. We study everything—time, sexual intercourse, art, their structures. . . . Everything lends itself to scientific investigation, everything fills a cognitive function. If I were to define the mind of this era, I would call it an era analyzing itself while in the process of becoming, which process is in turn modified by the process of self-analysis. It seems to me that your field, psychosociology, is a fairly typical example. In a certain sense . . . it deepens one's understanding of things, but in another it makes them still heavier to bear.

Chapter 3

I WAS GOING to return to question seven, but when I picked up the questionnaire I happened to notice question sixteen. *Do you often go to the theater? to the movies? How often, on average, during the year? What is your opinion of the present trends of the theater, of the cinema? Would you please name the productions, directors, and actors that you enjoy . . .* And so on. This is quite interesting because I have, in fact, just been to see an English film, a thriller, fairly well done, with a murderer as the main character. A murderer whose side one comes to take, despite all one's principles. I was suddenly surprised to find myself wishing that nobody would prevent him from committing his next murder, the poisoning of a little girl. And I was not the only one. The entire theater wished him success. We all wanted evil to escape punishment. There is something muddy-minded about that. One can argue, of course—the excellent acting, the man's physical appearance . . . The murderer had all the qualities of a man worthy of the name: courage, intelligence, and so on. And what is more, he was a superb horseman. The audience was *on his side*. In spite of all, the fact remains mysterious. Two hours spent under the spell of evil, the overthrowing of the great ethical choices: justice, compassion, charity. What if that had been years instead of hours, and if there had been not two hundred specta-tors but two hundred thousand, two million, twenty million—what then? In those two hours staked on the victory of the devil there was a certain yearning, a certain availability.

When all is said and done, do not the lies and crimes of despots show up for what they are to everyone, and in the same way? Yes, are not those crimes committed quite publicly with everybody aware of them? When the masses applaud a rationalist executioner or a criminal genius, they long for the triumph of what amounts to a . . . criminal providence. They are on the side of the knife. Up to the very end. Sometimes even up to their own end. The superman fails or perishes, the screen goes dark, the lights come on. Usually there is a moment of embarrassment. Not that it cannot be explained. The action makes us accomplices of the hero's will, even if he is a murderer instead of a hero. If he were a sheriff in a western and the story unfolded according to his will, everyone would similarly wish for the triumph of justice.

And so I go to the theater—for professional reasons; but I also go to films—on average, four or five times a month. As for the theater, although I have been involved in it for such a long time, I am at present going through a critical period, I feel a kind of weariness. I believe less and less in the theater in an age when there is no longer any spiritual conception of life. For another thing, a man on stage, his voice, his gestures, his physical presence seem to me too real—it feels like a kind of assault. The theater today has destroyed its old convention, which until today was invisible, that is to say, it has lost its very essence, its secret. Avant-garde trends and experiments have in-troduced a convention within a convention. Perhaps it is an attempt—a very ambitious one—which directors and authors are making in order to find a new way out. But this foreign body is still there, the actor's person, his face, his legs, and his clearly nonconventional arms, his sweat, his hair, the grinding of his teeth and his hoarseness. Someone, I believe, defined the theater as the only art which does not leave a corpse behind it. Admittedly, performances do not get hung on a wall like pictures in a museum, nor do they stack up like books along library shelves—they lose their material substance the moment they are over. The observation is pertinent, but nevertheless, there is a corpse left behind. Latterly, when I have been working in a theater, I have sometimes had the feeling that I was doing an experiment on a dead organism, galvanized into life by laboratory techniques— a body cut up into little pieces and put together again in a different way: pieces of dead flesh that someone had connected up with "new" pieces, "innovative" pieces. My work reminded me sometimes of Dr. Barnard's transplants. In short, I fear that the search for a new mode of expression has deprived the stage of its mystery and that the theater no longer creates an illusion. Like the mass, which once used to be theater and possessed similar mysteries. Now, the mass is broadcast over the air, and actors likewise are increasingly with us through television and films. I'm getting used to it. Perhaps man, the three-dimensional body of man, has become too physical for me, as if exaggeratedly true. Especially during a period when I am overworking. His presence seems "anti-hygienic" to me. I experience it as an assault, as I've said, which forces me to choose one or another line of conduct, when above all else I would like rest and relief from this crowd, this noisy multitude, and I would be satisfied with a human shadow moving on television glass or movie cloth. So then, I go to a film as to an appointment with life. I do not know whether I am quite up on all its current tendencies and present trends, but what attracts me there is simple: the cinema has not given up believing in life. Its measure of all things is reality, what happens to man among men. It doubts this neither in what it admires nor in what arouses its disgust—no more than did the novel of a while ago. It believes in life while the theater has put its faith in art and seeks artistic transcendence.

No, I do not prophesy, I am not a futurist, these are just ideas which are going through my head. We are not living in a century of great syntheses, we lack the ideas that create order among things. Everything is chaotic, spasmodic. The whole of contemporary culture puts me in mind of a melting pot where matter is seething and bubbles rise to surface, burst, and disappear. Is it not all going to boil over and then pour out in an irresistible stream, which will sweep away our cities and leap up skyward?—to unite and bring salvation in a single Word-Thought-Form-Tone? It will then turn out that we have spent our lives in a kingdom of wretched imbeciles. Can culture ever exist without the blessing of a universal certainty? Outside the universal Church? There have always been close links between theaters and temples.

Why am I talking about all this? To tell the truth, I don't know. Yes, perhaps I do. I think I said that in my early student days, I was crazy about the theater and used to take jobs as an extra. One of my friends, who had become tired of doing the same thing, had recommended to me a friend of his who was a director. Soon after this at the university I had a walk-on part in an English psychological play set in thirteenth-century Flanders. Then I played a farmhand in *The Wedding*, wearing a woolen cloak and carrying a scythe. That was a somewhat mad period of my life. I was living in a truly disinterested fashion—no self-seeking, but taking with one hand and throwing away with the other. I was following my bent, my curiosity. Which is not to say that I did not respect the rules of the game, but I already had my own private, personal rules. I quit the law for philosophy. I felt free.

By that time I was no longer living with my parents. For not long before, in the middle of Christmas dinner, my father, as was his custom, had begun to recite by heart the death scene of Podbipieta during the siege of Zbaraz. I had endured this ritual for many years but this time, after he began to choke up and his eyes filled with tears, I could not stand it any longer. With sadistic calm, I launched into a description of the various periods when our cavalry had the duty of "pacifying" the Ukrainian countryside. Then, immediately afterward, I described the recent visit of Goebbels to Marshal Pilsudski. There ensued a terrible scene. My father came at me with his stick. Even while I was struggling, I scanned his face, apoplectic with rage and riddled with spasms. I was sorry for him but, catching my breath, I went on with my harangue: unemployment, rigged elections, etc. A few days later I found a cheap little room and unearthed some private pupils to tutor. Later, of course, I was reconciled with my father, but from that time on I lived alone. My life during that period was "purer," I was less susceptible than I am today to that sort of blackmail that we are subject to when appeal is made to our "knowledge of what has to be." I didn't know so much. The laws of economics and history, the meaning of life and death, just like my own prospects and the cut of my jacket, all left me rather cold. I made friends with a girl prompter who was also a Jehovah's Witness. If I remember correctly, my view of man was that he represented one of the forms of universal existence—an "existential" essence; that is, having the ability to become embodied in a substance. I frequented the troupes in rehearsal and made contacts in the acting world. The extras and second-raters spent time in a certain café where I enjoyed a certain popularity, the kind that is bestowed on pleasant-mannered idlers, especially when they are more inclined to listen than to speak. I came within an ace of turning into one of those good fellows, one of those characters who hang around the theaters and were found on the small prewar stages. A few of them have survived, like insects pinned to a board. That kind of life had its charms. There is something about the theater that is less everyday than reality, even in its everyday and hardworking aspects. Now, that atmosphere of the circus, of camaraderie and of art as a sanctuary has for the most part disappeared. The element of fantasy has vanished, to be replaced by management and administration. Often I would play billiards with the actors. They were a scandalous little community. I was interested in their mythomania and their showing off, in their lack of real seriousness—that is what I liked about them: their lack of seriousness, which they made believe was deliberate—and conscientious. Any one of them would have sold his soul for a funny story—that is the blessed truth, they adored having fun! But at the same time, they were more genuine than other people, they evinced all the human weaknesses, and I came to realize that although it was their job to pretend, when it came down to it, their make-believe was far less than that of so-called sober characters. On stage they played gods, profligates, kindly uncles, and through each new character they have become familiar with the complexity of mankind. They enacted all the forms of sin and virtue, they changed their faces, voices, and behavior from night to night and finally got to a point beyond which Being and Nothingness are found: everything is true and nothing is false, everything is false and nothing true. Beyond that point there is no shame. I believe they were free from the shame of living, like everything in nature except man. In one of Shakespeare's plays—I don't remember which, perhaps you will know—someone says: Shame affords the fool a safe refuge. There is a humble sense of weakness, a despairing pride in that line; only an actor could have written it. For hours on end I could watch their gestures and their mimicry, which amounted to a pastiche of real drama or tragicomedy—and which they never noticed or felt as unimportant.

I got to know one of them better than the others, a man with pale eyes who always smiled. He was a somewhat eccentric character, not an especially good actor, but one who held a place of some note in theatrical circles, a world he scorned to a certain extent—in short, a "fascinating personality," as they say. I never knew why he liked me, or if he actually did. At first, I suspected him of being a homosexual; it was his delicate bone structure and plumpness that gave me that impression. He had small hands and feet. After rehearsals he would invite me to ride with him in a carriage in Lazienki Park and he used to tell me, for example, that he was the only true impotent male in all of Poland! He maintained, in fact, that impotence did not exist, except for a few rare cases caused by a kick from a horse; impotence was only a fiction invented by women neglected by their husbands. He held actors very cheap and reminded me that until recently they could not be buried in consecrated ground. His tone of voice was confidential, muffled, and somewhat nasal, and out of the blue, he would urge me to give up the university and enroll in a drama school. To him, an actor's talent consisted in physical magnetism. I remember his words: "A good actor is but the charm of his physique." He was likable but there was about him an air of strangeness, secrecy, and the chameleon nature, which he concealed under intelligent remarks—a kind of inconsistency, at once studied and arrogant. I was never sure when he began a sentence whether he knew how it would end.

You are surprised, no doubt, that I have strayed so far from the subject, but despite appearances this digression is relevant to question number seven, to which I mean to return. Do you remember what I said at the beginning of the first tape? I said that I, too, was expecting something from myself; namely, the elucidation of a few questions which remain obscure. One of them had to do with this man, whom I liked a great deal, whom I admired, even, to a certain extent, and whom, to a certain extent also, I still pity. He was killed during the occupation, by bullets from *my* gun, but it was he who headed for his own ruin. I think that at bottom he was not really bad. What, after all, is a really bad man? Perhaps someone who considers all other men bad and commits evil in order to forestall, or defend himself against, the universal evil which he anticipates. That seems to me an attitude which is not so much the result of a rational conviction as the product of fear, despair, and hatred. It happens, however, that a man may consider himself worse than other men when he carries within him a soft, putrifying core that poisons him from inside. He then tries to conceal it from others and from himself. That often works, especially in periods when nothing special is happening. But sometimes it does not work, when the times, as they say, are uncertain. I think that was the case here. But I will come back to this when I deal with one of the subsections of question seven:

Have you ever made a decision which you consider to

40

be the decision of a free man, that is, a decision entirely free from constraint, free from any convention or from conditioning of a collective kind? Did you act upon this decision?

The answer is: "Yes." At least once I made and acted on a decision of this sort. Was it an entirely free decision? At the time I made it, definitely—if only for the reason that I was going against all social conditioning and conventions. Does that in itself mean that it was the decision of a free man? As I said: at the time I made it, yes.

I don't want to speak in riddles, so I will try to make it brief—as far as possible, of course. I shan't be able to avoid going into personal matters, but—who knows?—with the help of this drink of whiskey . . .

I've already spoken about my joining the Resistance. For ten months I drilled a group of high-school boys in the handling of a gun and the use of hand grenades. Then for a time I operated a radio transmitter from a cellar in the Zoliborz quarter. In March 1943 I began to train some new recruits, this time in the tactics of street warfare. The question of free choice did not arise. There was no room for "I want" or "I don't want." It has been said of the Poles that one may certainly ask whether they are in possession of all their five senses but that they surely have a sixth: the collective instinct of national defense. That's what I meant by saying that I never felt a doubt. I felt it to be a glaring necessity, at the same time as I was angered by the required Polish heroics. It would seem that my "self" in the singular was the prisoner of a large collective "self" whose uproar had deafened my conscience. My father could be proud of me; I had become the worthy heir of his own heroes. Who knows, he may have been right and I may, in fact, have inherited the family genes. Despite the scenes I had made at home, perhaps my main psychical axis was as if aligned with the upright of the national cross, but the wrong way up, so to speak.

I thought over the campaign of 1939 with a clear enough mind. From the first shot to the last, Poland defended herself for thirty-eight days. If the Russian army had not intervened on September 17, the Resistance would undoubtedly have continued all of two months. Neither France nor Belgium nor even the British expeditionary force held out for so long. For a nonindustrial country, unprotected by geography, and which had no training in modern warfare, and—what is more—which was being attacked from two sides, there was no reason to be ashamed. The outcome could not have been different. I remember that I was at the Legia pool sunbathing when the loudspeakers announced the news of the Ribbentrop-Molotov pact. Despite the August heat I felt a sudden chill. Nor did I cherish any illusions later on. The chances that an armed conflict could succeed under the conditions existing during the occupation seemed very slim to me, at least as far as overall strategy was concerned. No military operation on the part of the Resistance could, I thought, affect the final outcome of the war. And as you know, the losses were enormous. The Resistance movement as a whole, regardless of the politics of its members, favored military action. The graduating classes were furnishing an army of adolescents; the students in the underground classrooms went straight into courses on railway sabotage. I watched this happen with mixed emotions, while I continued to train my recruits. For the most part they followed the tradition of *Polishness* in remaining ignorant of world affairs. They came to grief in the streets or in the death camps or else were torn to bits by dogs during interrogations. They died without any idea of the structure of the society to come—clinging to the most elementary notions of liberty and justice. When I would raise for them the issue of agrarian reform or the problem of public institutions they would eventually come back at me with a vague: "They'll take care of that after the war." For them, these problems would be solved by others, later. Issues were never brought up during the underground classes or briefings. Up above there was an anonymous high command, and they—they were the army. I had the feeling that if there was an army and a command, there ought to be a battle. And there was. Two hundred fifty thousand people died in it, along with their city. If my father were still alive, he would not like to talk about it. Obviously many reasons, or rather many motives, exist for keeping oneself from passing judgment—considerations infinitely delicate, complex in the extreme. Indeed, I myself hesitate to broach this topic, possibly out of *respect* for its complexity, and because I, too, may have a dose of national tact, which in Poland dictates that the greatest flashes of insight must never be expressed. But what I want to talk about goes back to an earlier date.

In September 1943, I suggested to a certain young woman that she join the organization. I had known her for several years. Originally from the country, she had been admitted to the Warsaw conservatory three months before the outbreak of hostilities. My relationship to this woman was very important to me; in fact, for a while it took precedence over everything else. In bringing her into the Resistance I had a definite goal, neither, as you will see, entirely patriotic nor altogether self-serving. A few weeks earlier, one of her close relations had died at Auschwitz. Since then she had virtually gone out of her mind. She had begun to drink and, between drinking bouts, to seek contacts with the Resistance. I knew that she would find them. Getting in touch would be easy, especially for her: she was a waitress in the Melpomena café, where I had worked as a coatroom attendant. It was a place frequented by people in the most diverse occupations, such as my friend, the actor with the pale eyes whom I mentioned. But that is not the point. I knew that the café was a meeting place for various underground groups. Now, I was convinced that she was one of those people who are least fit for undercover work. She was rather scatterbrained, too ambitious, and at the same time too confiding. She was one of those women whom in society one would describe as "delightfully crazy," and with whom, if you meet them at the seaside—which in fact is where I had come to know her—you can swim very far out; they are not afraid of getting in over their heads.

At the time I'm talking about, I was unable to view her objectively; I chalked many things up to her eccentric character, the usual thing in talented people. And talent she had. But I also know that she was one of those girls who get themselves recruited by secret services. Assailed by grim forebodings, I would imagine her by turns abandoned to police dogs and raped by officers of the Gestapo. For two weeks I listened to her confessions until the day when she told me about a new acquaintance she had just made. It was in September 1943; it was her day off and we were in a bistro on Mazowiecka Street. After a glass of vodka I told her that she could be useful to us. She was impressed by the *us*. It had never occurred to her that I could concern myself with anything other than her little self. She instantly agreed. My role, on the other hand, was much more difficult. I had to invent a fiction, to create likelihoods. A word with Rabczyn would have sufficed to get her a real "contact," but since I was quite determined not to bring that about, there was only one solution: to attach her to an organization which did not exist. This is the decision, the "free decision" I referred to when I said "yes" a moment ago.

Regardless of how the story ends, I believe that on that occasion I performed an act of individual liberty; that on that occasion, at least, I experienced a moment of freedom. All this must seem a bit strange and incoherent to you. I quite understand. But I knew what I was doing. I had fought for three years in the Resistance, I was well aware of the price one is sometimes induced to "pay" in clandestine organizations. It's not the kind of thing shown in the movies, and former fighters don't talk about it.

I have already made it clear that I couldn't avoid raising personal problems. Indeed, do problems that are not personal even exist? No matter what we talk about, we betray ourselves by the subjects that we pass by; they show what we're afraid of and what gives us pain. But keeping quiet doesn't merely betray us. Nothing is more difficult than to keep quiet. I have always admired those who have mastered the art—knowing how to remain silent. That almost amounts to keeping for oneself "the ownership of oneself." Have you ever noticed how extremely difficult it is not to answer a question? We talk because speech is our way of being, and through words we prove to ourselves that we exist. But we also deliver ourselves into the hands of strangers. That is precisely what I have been doing for three days. While the tape is turning, I never stop having an ambiguous feeling: the satisfaction of falling into a trap. The temptation is very great. Take, for example, the issues raised in questions twelve through fifteen, which in my opinion constitute a sort of "metaphysical core." No questions could be more personal. One of them is put this way: *Do the ethical rules you apply in your life contain a religious element? In your thoughts and your actions do you take into consideration the possibility of an "afterlife" (based, for example, on rewards and punishments), and do you associate the idea of God with the notion of Good and Evil?* Those are words that remind me of the first "lesson" given to candidates for an Arctic expedition: "You will not find the test difficult; all you have to do is to come back alive."

During the many interrogations I was subjected to after 1945, I was made to define my politico-ideological position of before and after the war. I was asked a dozen times or more to write down the story of my life in detail; and whenever I gave them any new piece of information, I had to start over again from the beginning. I came back alive from those investigations, which, as everybody knows, is unusual. The questions dealt primarily with my ties to the various organizations of the period. During the questioning I had the impression that the whole business was not so much about me as about a typical case intended to confirm a hypothesis made up in advance. Luckily, it turned out that I wasn't completely typical, just to the extent, perhaps, that I stubbornly kept insisting that my behavior resulted from my metaphysical commitments. When I was asked why I had joined the organization in 1940, I replied: "Because I believed in God." I think they ended up thinking I was mad, and yet, all things considered, my activity in the Resistance *was* based on ethico-religious beliefs. The reality of Evil, during those years, was blatant; the nature of the Good had become unmistakable. Problems such as the meaning of life or one's attitude toward death had never before been so simple as during that period when black was absolutely distinct from white. Perhaps a world has to end first. On the day before the beginning of the war, people were quietly waiting for their streetcars; young women, tanned by vacation sunshine, were wearing thin, colorful dresses. Not long ago I read a description of Warsaw on the morning of August 31. The writer remembered a number of details, among others a pretty passenger touching up her makeup in a streetcar. Up to the very last minute, the present looked real, then, suddenly, it went to pieces. When a milk bar where one would regularly drink one's kefir comes to be used as shelter for people who had just been wounded, that means that a certain reality will never return. And that's how it was—the moment when time explodes, when one is petrified by the ease with which the succession of days and years comes to a halt. It only takes a few puffs of wind for the lights to go out and for broken panes to start crunching underfoot. The next day, the life one had known seems like an optical illusion. But, I repeat, perhaps these things are useful, perhaps they enable us to reconsider the possibility of the afterlife. There's another easy test for you—all you have to do is to come back alive. And sometimes one does come back . . . Yes, I really joined the Resistance so as to fight against the Devil. But that kind of explanation was not so readily accepted, after the war.

Chapter 4

TODAY'S SESSION was devoted to reading some reports. Then we had some discussion, and I have just come from taking a shower. But I'm very much afraid that this evening I shan't be able to collect my thoughts. I don't know what to start with or what I ended with yesterday. It seems to me I must have been talking about . . . Ah yes, that's it, the war. What weather they have here! Will this fierce salt wind never stop blowing? The effect it has can be melodramatic. At the height of the storm this afternoon, a Frenchman was speaking to us. In his remarks—very good by the way—the speaker was praising the courage which attends humanity in its present-day efforts and achievements. He called them "dizzying" and "terrifying"—in short, a sermon in the heartthrob intellectual style of the Parisians. He wound up with a story from his student days when he used to go mountain climbing. He had, for his most difficult climbs, the services of a guide by the name of Ringele who had the strength and stature of a giant. When they were scaling a particularly steep rock face, and he, the city man, started to get vertigo and shouted: "Ringele, my head is spinning!" the giant would reply, "Well, then, let it spin!"—*"Schwindel' frei!"* and he'd draw him up with a pull on the rope. No doubt the Frenchman meant to say that when we feel dizzy at the sight of the abyss opening at our feet and want to step back because our heads are spinning, we should shout to each other, "Well, let it—*Schwindel' frei!*" A fine metaphor. And to spice the whole thing, imagine the wind howling outside the window all during the speech! The Frenchman earned his well-deserved applause.

Let us go back to September 1943. It was about then that I first heard of murders being committed within the Resistance movement itself. There were whisperings of the activity of under-underground cells and secret trials, of rival factions within the groups settling their private accounts between themselves. In the east, the Germans were abandoning one city after another; the front was getting closer. The burning issue was, who was going to take over Poland? It was a difficult time. In the ranks of the Resistance the atmosphere thickened; everybody thought he smelled traitors everywhere. In my unit, a man was wrongly executed and the one in charge of the business disappeared as well. No one knew exactly where the denunciations were coming from—but it turned out that the man condemned was innocent. This was why I decided to keep my young woman out of the Resistance. I told her that she was going to work for an intelligence network that took orders direct from the High Command. I made it clear to her that the exceptional importance of the missions to be accomplished would force us to observe very strict security rules. I administered the oath to her myself. As her code name she chose "Mewa" (Seagull), no doubt in memory of a certain deserted beach.

At the outset, the hoax didn't present any insurmountable difficulties for me. I assigned "Seagull" to shadow an old lawyer about whom I knew nothing, except that he was harmless. One month later I knew his every movement, the names of all the people he had seen, the nature of all his affairs. She rented a room opposite his chambers. One day, she ran into him in the elevator, the next day he sent her flowers. Pretty work! After six weeks I knew for certain that our man had ties with the command of the Civilian Corps. I ordered Mewa to stop at once and move out. Some time later, I had to reprimand her: she had actually gone to his funeral without telling me—out of curiosity. The lawyer had been found in the elevator of his building; it could have been a heart attack. She told me the news herself and I did manage to conceal my surprise. She gazed at me admiringly. For her, there was not a shadow of doubt that I was acting a part to perfection. From that day on, I began to send her to the country with a suitcase filled with my old books—to a different town each time. She would check the suitcase at the Cracow or Lublin train station, mail the receipt to General Delivery in the same place, addressing the envelope to some nonexistent person, and take the next train back to Warsaw. I would usually choose her free days. I had trained her to follow the instructions that are given to all underground agents, right down to details of personal appearance. For women, no makeup, no contacts with strangers. In the event the train was searched, she was to say that the books were going to a secondhand book dealer (they were detective stories in several languages). I gave her to understand that the reports of "our network," which I called "Rondo," were in code in the books, in invisible ink. As for the rest, I barely allowed her to guess that it was information meant to reach London by different channels. Thus, while insuring safety, I was satisfying her most ardent ambition. Meanwhile, I was squandering suitcases. The friends from whom I extorted old fiber handbags were convinced that I was selling lard on the black market. That may seem funny today, but at the time those suitcases pursued me right into my dreams. Add to all this that Mewa's attention was not always wandering; she could be very perceptive in her intuitions. I had my work cut out to set the stage. There, too, there were no problems at the beginning. I would pay a delivery boy to bring me the suitcase at the appointed hour, having summoned Mewa to arrive a little earlier. The whole scene was played without a word; we called it "receiving the merchandise." (One time I made use of my father. He came at just the right moment with the suitcase, his gold-rimmed glasses, and his railroad engineer's cap. He had not been wearing it for very long and clearly considered it a particularly ingenious piece of camouflage.) Then I would send Mewa to the station.

Was I crazy? No, very simply, I did not want to lose her. I made my first mistake in February 1944. I felt sorry for her; she had lost weight, the trips were tiring her. I therefore decided to bring two new people into the network. Later, several others joined us. I organized secret meetings and finally solved the problem of the suitcases. I had the idea of using *only one*. My courier would escort it to the town of X, check it at the station, and toss an envelope with the receipt into a mailbox. After a certain lapse of time, another of my couriers would go to the same place, pick up the envelope at General Delivery, retrieve the bag from the station, and bring it back to Warsaw. It was a closed circuit. The symbolic contents of the suitcase would change according to the direction: old newspapers, *The Mystery of the Yellow Room*, and *The Perfume of the Woman in Black* would go on the outward journey as the secret reports of the "Rondo" network, and on the return journey, as instructions parachuted in by the High Command.

The critical phase occurred in April. It is only at the

end of a tragedy or a farce that events pile up with blinding speed. Two unknown men came to my rooms on the same day that I discovered my pistol had vanished from its hiding place. That same morning I had received a telephone call from Mewa, who wanted to see me to discuss an urgent matter. So I had two important meetings on that one day, both at the Melpomena café. The first lasted an hour. I was being pressured to rejoin the organization called "Thought and Action," and to furnish its leaders with the entire outfit of "Rondo." Three hours later Mewa returned my pistol and told me that someone who had been collaborating with the Gestapo had just been put out of harm's way. It was our old friend, the actor with the pale eyes and the fine bones. The two events were not linked in any way and yet my fiction worked itself out in a pair of shots. For the second shot was intended for me personally: the organization "Thought and Action" tried to kill me when I rejected their demands. The bullet grazed my shoulder. All this took place in the space of five days. "Rondo" suspended all activity. I still wonder why that name in particular had occurred to me.

To sum up: I had invented a fiction to keep danger at arm's length, and what I had invented was the very thing that brought it on. In making up the fiction I was free; in carrying it out I became enslaved. And lastly, I myself got caught in what I tried to escape. What's the conclusion?

None. I sent the panic-stricken girl back to her parents in the country. She was pregnant. Had it not been for the hoax I had perpetrated and its upshot, had it not been for the trauma that Mewa subsequently suffered, she would surely have died during the Uprising. She gave birth to a daughter. This actor who was trying to frighten her with stories about the Gestapo and to whom she was bound by ties stronger than friendship had knowledge of my contacts with Rabczyn. If he had not given himself away to her, he could have put the information to good use. As for those who took a shot at me, the idiots . . . Obviously another mistake. Instead of gaining time, I said outright exactly what I thought of them. With fury, even after ten years! Since my misadventure at the university, sure enough, ten years had elapsed but I could tell it was the same brutal rage, the same stick striking my head. Yet without those feelings I never would have decided to send Mewa away; I would have kept her with me, and that could have ended in disaster. As I said, *no conclusion*. But if it is true that mechanisms suppress freedom, I venture to think that chance is freedom hidden inside mechanisms.

Let me come back to the "metaphysical core." It is, after all, not a big jump. Between these various matters and the problem of freedom there is an organic link— indeed, a kind of identity. They all spring from a common source: the confusion of human and divine affairs. You must by now be aware that I settle my accounts by myself, alone. Don't worry, I'll take care to spare you embarrassing confessions. But tonight I am under the spell of this tape recorder which I'm addressing and of the wind outside rattling the windowpanes.

I said there was a kind of link between metaphysics and freedom. It definitely exists; let me develop the idea: the link exists most conspicuously between metaphysics and ethics, and its effective work is—amounts to— freedom. Is not "honesty" a metaphysical idea, does it not mean emancipation from the materialistic? Any human meanness is nothing more than a kind of slavery resulting from the lack of faith in a supra-material existence—dirty tricks are always atheistic. After the banning of

Forefather's Eve in Warsaw in March 1968, when students were arrested, the newspapers were teeming with lies and denunciations; I was horrified. I suddenly thought: those who think that baseness is profitable, because whatever happens everything always ends *here on earth*, are basically poor fools. We do not, in fact, know what *everything* is and we cannot know with any certainty where it ends—or even if it ends. You told me about the rediscovery of Hegel in the American universities. That is strange. I wonder what your students think of this brilliant German with water on the brain, who has contaminated half the planet with his demonic certainty which has become the curse of our age and that of socialism, too—millions of Smerdiakovs convinced that anything goes because God does not exist—Smerdiakovs who escape hanging.

What were those questions again? *Do the ethical rules you apply in your life contain a religious element? And do you associate the idea of God with the notion of Good and Evil?*

Yes, I think so. With one amendment on a particular point. "Rules"—that's too limiting a word. It would be better to say: "ethical endeavor." Moreover, the word *religious* for a secular being such as I, who lives outside the Church, means to me morality rather than anything else. And for me the moral sphere is inseparable from awareness. These questions, by the way, need going into at greater length. We can't do it now. To tell you the truth, some of the topics raised by your study are very awkward— define one's relationship with God, and in a few words! I am not a man of the Church, and yet. . . . Don't we use God's name too freely these days? Today, God is a rhetorical metaphor in literary essays. Perhaps we should avoid the expression. I would suggest another metaphor: "The Unknowable Principle of the Universe," for example.

If I must answer your question, then, it is yes once again. In my mind, my heart, and my hopes The Unknowable Principle of the Universe is associated with the notion of Good and Evil, and I believe that man's moral will is its reflection. But if I keep on talking about it, my words will end up covering me like poison ivy; I'll begin to swell up and to give off bubbles. In the face of the greatest mysteries, nobody has ever remained silent. On the other hand, too many have fallen into verbalism. It would surely be wiser for me to stick to my own story.

I've already spoken about my high-school friend—I shall call him Icz. After graduation, we both decided to study law. It was actually with him that I was walking in the university courtyard when the Jewish student was attacked. Icz was punched while he tried to defend me and he went with me to the hospital after my oral examination was over. We were good friends from classroom days and what is more, I had always admired his intelligence; he had read more than all of us put together. Along with the law, he was studying literature, and he passed everything with seemingly no effort. Later we saw less of each other. I knew that he wrote and that generally his head was full of new ideas. One day he read me a chapter of a study entitled "The Novel and Premeditation." If my memory serves me right, it was about the similarity between the creative imagination of the novelist and the creation of alibis by prospective criminals. I don't remember precisely his arguments, but some of them seemed to me original. Icz maintained, for example, that the famous women poisoners had plotted their crimes in the same way that great writers plot their novels, by working and reworking.

In both cases, he said, success consists in establishing the fiction, and that is achieved only by concealing the methods and devices and distracting the attention that might focus on the criminal-author. I mention this to give you an idea of what the man's mind was like. He was certainly not stupid. What surprised me was that his reaction after our disgusting misadventure was totally different from mine. I should say exactly the opposite of mine. He tried to explain that he was wondering whether those who had beaten us up might not be right. Right of course in a way that went beyond the act of violence they had committed, right in a more general way. At first I thought he had gone mad. He set out to explain to me their ideas—the platform of the radical nationalists of the day—and suddenly I realized that I was being addressed by a man under a spell. It was a little like an abnormal pregnancy, a fertilization that brings about a mutation of species. To understand the fanatic nature of the thing, you should imagine a friend who has turned into an owl, or a friend with the head of a horse or a fox, and, you should have known the friend as I had known him, through and through. I shall never forget that conversation. He talked to me about trade being in the hands of *foreigners*. Since he was sitting sideways to me I could see his eye naked, without the barrier of his lenses, his blue eye, dark and dreamy—and his Adam's apple moving up and down.

He always wore the collar of his shirt outside his jacket collar, à la Slowacki. I couldn't understand what he was saying, couldn't make head or tail of it. To me, political platforms were abstractions, and this one seemed to me sordid and absurd. By what path had this one penetrated the mind of so intelligent a man? It was a mystery. I nevertheless came to the conclusion—though not until right now—that the main driving force behind

57

Icz's intelligence was a deep-seated insecurity. He let any outside thought enter his head. Perhaps he was built like an open circuit. Perhaps he was open to all possible mental states. Perhaps all phenomena coming from the outside world seemed to him better than himself. I suspect that unconsciously he inclined toward uniting with a mode of thought broader than his own, and whose value might be confirmed by the future. It seems as if Icz was being constantly blackmailed by a truth which might not visit his mind and might come to pass without him. There are some people who panic at the thought that somewhere there is a party in full swing and they haven't been invited. For Icz, it was a little different. He was tortured by the possibility that he might not be invited to attend the new era. I was devastated. After our conversation I spent a bad night: Icz's words beset me in the darkness. I smoked one cigarette after another. Until that moment, I had never felt myself directly responsible for the fate of the country. I considered all that to be the concern of specialists, the political professionals. And here was my feeling suddenly turning against me. Was society going to adopt this sinister program? I had a premonition that it could happen. It had already happened in Italy and Germany. And if I was right, if matters were already so far advanced, that would mean my involvement in a monumental error. It was then that I lost all certainty: about myself, about my beliefs and recollections, about my father's integrity, about my memory, about tradition, about education. There in the darkness, I discovered the poor, mean, little, stupefied Polish reality. I was filled with fear and disgust.

Icz was a "conductor of timeliness" in the way that a copper wire is a conductor of electricity. He let the current of the era pass through him, he lent himself to incandescence, and he shone. Then he faded out. For several years, he hovered around the joiners, published articles which spoke of crises and renovation; then he was silent. He had been rejected. He spent the wartime in Poland. In February 1945, when I returned from the prison camp where I ended up after the Uprising, we spent an entire night at his house, talking by the light of a candle. He thought that the victory of Communism was the right thing, the result of the logic of events. During this conversation—we had no heat and were freezing in our overcoats and fur caps—Icz obliterated our past while I listened, puffing on a pipe filled with cigarette tobacco. At one point, he started explaining that we had been prepared from childhood to live in a society based on lies. He said: "We were already corrupted during our years at school." I let him talk, though the blood rushed to my head. I could see the priest, with his bony profile and hooked nose, shuttling back and forth between his desk and the blackboard, explaining to us that the Greeks knew all about life and the Romans all about power. For a moment, I felt as if I were back there, sitting in the second row, next to the window, with a view of the schoolyard. To my left I had a square patch of sky crisscrossed by the branches of a maple, and in front of me, bent over and etched with a fine point, the studious profile of Icz. No, in that distant time we were innocent.

We spoke of many other things. Icz seemed to have neither eaten nor slept during the whole war. He only thought and thought. From the war he had deduced a whole set of new ideas. Thanks to one of them he accounted for the defeat, namely that Poland had been invented by the Germans in the ninth or tenth century as a buffer to protect them against attack from the east.

From the beginning, Poland had been conceived of as a bulwark. This role had been forced upon her at the same time as had Christianity, and it was according to the same principle that she had been granted independence after the First World War. According to Icz, this maneuver already held the seeds of the weakness, the inadequacy, the subjection that were to bring on the destruction of the nation and its life. Of course, I am summarizing. Icz also explained the defeat of 1939 by the emptiness of our social relations during the prewar period, by the fictional nature of a state bloated with historical vanity. He argued that Pilsudski was aware of this "Polish unreality" and that he had tried, with full consciousness of the facts, to provide the country with an element of independence. He wanted to create an illusion of power by means of anachronisms and legends so as to make up for the material foundations that we lacked and could not supply. According to Icz, Pilsudski understood that a country crippled by centuries of servitude had to have some form of spiritual greatness imposed upon it; the backwardness of the country must be transformed through imagination. Icz called this "the reality of the unreal," and thought that it was the only hope *for now*. It was a renaissance on the psychic level, that is, in dreams, obsessions, and collective myths—in spirit rather than substance. To tell the truth, I felt surprise tinged with approval, because this idea strictly considered showed on his part a challenging perceptiveness. Anyhow, it's of no importance; he himself certainly has no recollection of it.

It is not by mere chance that I call up these memories, by the way. What I have just been talking about relates to those questions in your study which have to do with the human personality. It's a fundamental theme. The questionnaire asks me who I am, so I must define myself in relation to myself, declare how I conceive freedom, what my conscience is and what my heaven. All this is too tremendous, each question towers as high above me as Mount Ararat. Yet at times I tell myself that I possess more experience than these questions contain—or more simply, that I am different from the people who thought them up. We have a different past and a different present, and our experience of life differs to a considerable degree. I sometimes have the impression that each of us inhabits a separate hemisphere of consciousness. There must be many things which American scholars know better than I. There also are things about which I know more than they do. What does this come to? Not a great deal. At most, it means that each of us pursues his own fate in his own world. But we both make the same mistake. When we look at the other hemisphere of experience, we judge it according to our own. It is sometimes difficult for us to understand one another. When we say "table," "dog," "wheel," we both mean approximately the same thing. With words like "town" or "house," differences begin to crop up. But when we say "man," "right," "freedom," are we still talking about the same things? I assume that you imagine a free person, and the rights that belong to him. I see for my part someone who no longer knows his own rights and who is kept at a distance from freedom. Perhaps your train of thought is marked by excessive optimism and mine by a painful and equally excessive sensitivity. Two hemispheres of experience, and a different consciousness.

If I am not mistaken, I said yesterday that I had begun to believe in God in 1940; that is correct. But after the war, I began to believe in History.

I mean by that a certain intellectual and moral condition having practically nothing in common with faith as a religious experience. It is a condition close to hypnosis, perhaps—almost magical. It is the making over of one's values to the bank of time. It is a kind of franchise granted not altogether deliberately, yet not under compulsion, and essentially disinterested. Many people have performed this change on their own persons. I am talking about honest people, each of whom must have experienced the loss of his inner identity and a state of self-refutation—sooner or later. Not to understand this is not to know one of the least clear of human truths, the least clear, perhaps, for those very people who have experienced it. Nor must one forget *when* they experienced it: after the war. The war gave everyone the sense of great inner integrity; at that time the boundaries between "yes" and "no" were clearly defined. I have already talked about that. In those days, everybody knew who he was. If I claim that I was a believer then . . . Yes, the occupation had a metaphysics of its own; it was like passing from one realm of existence to another. I felt that my life could change utterly; I was expecting the ultimate, triumphant revelation. I would live the End and the Beginning.

The war still haunts my dreams at times. Dreams are the best way of celebrating the past, but today the newspaper, television, and the cinema do a competent job of it. And there are, of course, committees in charge of observing the memorial days. The day I was leaving Warsaw, while I was waiting for a taxi, suitcase in hand, a drunk was standing twenty paces from me in front of a plaque dedicated to the victims of Nazism. Staggering, he stared at it intently, stubbornly, and with the unction of a drunkard on the stage, he waved his hat through the air to make the sign of the cross. Then he fell across the sidewalk in the posture of a man who has been shot. I looked around to see if anyone was watching this macabre spectacle, but there was nobody. Apparently, nobody had noticed anything. You see, I live in an odd country—a country where thousands of people have a car, where tens of thousands are saving up in order to buy a car, and where millions dream of owning a car; where these same people stand in line for hours to buy some meat; a country where one spends a whole night in front of the box office of a theater to buy a ticket; where drunken tourists are taken in buses to see the sites of former exterminations. An odd country, which never forgets its past, but which more often than not does not understand it. This drunk I saw must have been about thirty. The two boys with long hair who were waiting for a taxi next to me must have been about nineteen. What could they understand, individually or together, of the forties or the fifties? Nothing. Almost nothing.

Chapter 5

FIFTH EVENING. Now that I have reached the postwar years, something important calls for mention: the inner split that I began to feel soon after my return from prison camp in 1945. I think of it as being double in self-contradiction. It was a kind of disturbance I had never before experienced, a confusion of all the pros and cons—a painful state, similar to the feeling that one is at odds with the law—and on a fundamental issue, that of one's personal dignity. At that time I had no steady work. My day began with a cup of dishwater coffee in a café improvised among bombed-out buildings. The friends I met were castaways, the old streets were corridors heaped with rubble. I made the trip from the Mokotów quarter to the center of town in an old truck full to bursting. Everything had changed: newspapers, addresses, bureaus and offices, the names of institutions. Everything was hurried, chaotic, improvised. Everything—except the dominating idea which thundered throughout the ruins announcing the regime newly established and the downfall of the old. Loudspeakers had been installed amid the debris. Some friends I met were in the depths of despair, others full of enthusiasm, but in all of them I could sense something like a flaw in metal. At the heart of their despair lay a deep-seated, anxious uncertainty as to the correctness of their beliefs; and in the others' enthusiasm, it was the tearing pain of breaking the last few embarrassing ties. I understood them alike, I felt as if split between them. When I was summoned for my first interrogation I had already been working in the theater for several months. I went on foot. The tree-lined streets were covered with dead leaves. As I walked along, I had the feeling of being made up of two parts, my yes's and my no's hooked together and clashing terribly. That was the time when they were arresting the former fighters of the Armia Krajowa at the same moment as they were carrying out the agricultural reform. I walked, my mind entirely preoccupied with this double thought. I did not know when I would return, what I was going to be asked, or how I should answer. I experienced only the tiredness of my double thought and a boredom with the self I had ceased to know.

For the first time, anxiety seized hold of me with the question: Was I still the person that I had been, the same entity that I had called "me" for thirty years? That *something* so close, so clear to myself, a little mysterious but also as simple as the fact of breathing, this same whole and original self, the same self that I had always been? I remember that moment perfectly. It must have been the first stage of the unhinging process. I was reproducing myself by division. I was secreting a new part of myself, foreign, yet mine, a second self.

I say that I remember that moment well. But I may be wrong, my memory may have hit upon that moment out of many others. In fact, the split probably came about by degrees, over a fairly long stretch. And I was not the only one. I have mentioned the friends I happened to meet in devastated Warsaw; I have spoken about their various reactions to what was happening in Poland. This split among us had an official definition: with us or against us, ally or enemy—sharp as the firing of a machine gun over a ditch. The loudspeakers bellowed it across the ruins fit to make themselves hoarse. It was like a power drill piercing our eardrums and our brains. The ditch was already dug deep. I met many of these people in the years that followed, and I still run into them sometimes. It is perfectly clear to me that if people held such widely diverging positions, it did not result from a difference in their intellectual ability or moral standards. If honest and sensible people were all on one side, and stupid and evil ones on the other, everything would be simple, but it is not simple. My daughter cannot understand it. But I know what I am talking about. I lived through the perplexities of both sides: those who joined the party and those who kept quiet during meetings, or shut themselves up at home. I understood their arguments, their doubts. That is how I know what I am talking about. At bottom, there is only one type of man I do not understand, that I have never understood—the cruel, blunt, and narrow—who hates any kind of hesitation, scruple, or uncertainty. No, nothing is more demonic than mediocrity. To be sure, mediocrity, which today is shamelessly adroit, was then fanatical and ruthless, but it is always the same organized force of vulgarity, as destructive in those days when it was armored in medals as today in its blatant cynicism. I therefore leave that type out of account. In everything I am trying to say here, I am talking about another kind of man, the only ones I am interested in, those who—independently of their beliefs and political orientations—are bound together by a fundamental sense of human dignity and responsibility; or simply by a certain coherence among their reasoned convictions; or even those who preserve a serious attitude toward serious things, toward themselves, society, and the world. But they, Poland, the world, everything was shaken, off balance. In the change that had overtaken Poland, some saw foreign annexation and political rape; others, a plan for reform on a national scale, social equality. You are no doubt wondering what determined whether an individual would rally to one or the other of these points of view . . .

It depended in large part on the internal center of gravity, on its location. In general, the new order was accepted by those who were bound to the traditions of the left, of the radical and secular intelligentsia, of enlightened rationalism, of the peasant and proletarian movements. It was rejected by those who had been brought up in the other traditional stream, non-revolutionary, bourgeois, or landed, which carried with it another conception of the nation, of national or Catholic unity. Of course, that is to draw a rather hasty, superficial dividing line. I could name former nationalists who after the war held positions in the government, and former socialists who at the same time were moldering in prison. I might add that after 1945 my compatriots of the "Thought and Action" movement averred themselves Christian Communists. But that is another story, because my aim, I repeat, is to stick to those people whose motives were pure. When one has such motives, one must pay the price. Some were accused of "past-mindedness" and "reactionary thought," others of opportunism and of treason to themselves. Well, the "reactionary thought" could have come from the Old Left's resentment at being rebuffed, or by the memory of the execution of Polish prisoners at Katyń. As for "opportunism," it might be the intellectual's regret or an imaginary hope. Sometimes also, remaining inflexible could be entirely the result of being a small shopkeeper. On either side of the ditch, after much blood had run into it, different people took their stand for different reasons. And none of them are today what they were then. All have changed. Time has done its work on everyone, which may well be what gives most food for thought: in what way have people changed? How has the new time machine done its work?

For years, my daughter and I have argued this point. It is the only one on which we cannot agree—our discussions always degenerate into arguments, even though I am a rather even-tempered man and she is an intelligent girl. A woman, in fact. She was born in 1944. In March 1945, I brought her from Kielce back to Warsaw. I took her from two old people, Mewa's parents—Mewa had been captured during a raid and sent to a work camp in Germany almost immediately after giving birth. I decided to play the role of father at a time when I did not even have an apartment, just a rented room in the Mokotów quarter. I took her to Warsaw in her baby basket. The train was not heated. I did not know where her mother was—Mewa was not found for another three months—and I racked my brains during the entire trip, wondering if I would know how to feed a very young infant. One of the items in your questionnaire goes like this: *What do you consider the greatest success of your life?* Certainly this was it—that night on the train, when, trembling with fear, I held on my knees, in the dark, this warm little living parcel, the little six-month-old Mewa— and the years that followed, the fact of having brought her up. The last time we had an argument was the day before I left. She shouted: "How could you have kept silent?" Mewa is a geologist, her husband a physicist in electronics. He does not like to discuss things outside his field; and the past is not his field. It is I who am responsible for the past, and anyhow, it is with me that fundamental issues are discussed; the husband is taciturn. The morning of my departure she did not look well. She was seated on the rug near the record player. I was just about to leave. I believe it was easier for her to part with me than with Bach. Having noticed her sad expression, I spoke first, although to tell the truth there was nothing to say. She is highly strung, passionate, absent-minded, although possessed of a kind of intense attention. When she was summoned to an interrogation, six years ago, after *Forefather's Eve* was banned at the National Theater and incidents occurred at the university, she was perfectly calm. I remember that then, too, she was sitting on the rug near the phonograph. Before going out she hid little multicolored capsules of Elenium and Valium in the seams of her corduroy slacks. For me, the Brandenburg Concertos will always be associated with those March mornings.

Why did I keep silent? Because I had come to the conclusion that History was right. Whatever I had thought and done until then was beginning to lose its importance in my mind, as if I were being wiped away by the gigantic, growing shadow of a colossus called the dialectic of change. A nervous curiosity made me read Marx and Lenin. I wanted to find in the original sources what this logic was that was undermining the foundations of my mind. Strange reading, supplying both the machinery and the key—a universal machine engaging all the gears at once—theories, arguments, and conclusions put together coherently: all you had to do was press a button and everything was explained—events, culture, religion, poverty, wealth, wars between nations, and relationships between men. But this universal explanation left one behind questionless. The result of accounting for everything was to preclude any possibility of evolution, and so the system of thought is petrified through its own answers—it's a sort of suicide by certainty. In a world that is explained and with a self that is explained, man is reduced to silence in the midst of a truth that is explained.

Absolute utopias, as we all know, feed the longing for a perfect universal order. And I, while busy reading, was also caught up in a reality being transformed; that is, I was in touch with real, day-to-day changes, planned and conceived in relation to a program for the total transformation of life, done in the name of the great original motives—liberty, equality, justice. The Word was in action. It filled the void left by "the illusions of the intellectuals" and "bourgeois morality." It was the language of the press and radio. The West called it "brainwashing," but oddly enough, this talk hit the bull's-eye in one respect: it was arousing a certain uneasiness. I did not feel responsible either for colonialism or for gas chambers, though I lived in a world where they were in operation. And that was enough. In such a world, no one could be altogether clean. After the war, when for the first time in my life I attended the premiere of a play that I had directed, everything—the famous actors, the play, the set—everything seemed to me boring and slapdash. All during the performance I had a feeling of uneasiness, a confused feeling that the actors on stage were pretending that they were acting, while I was pretending to be myself in a real theater. The curtain, the footlights, and the spotlights were also pretending. I think everybody realized it. We were all in the same boat and had to make the same shameful confession. Articles and speeches threw this shame back onto the past and onto those who had accepted it, namely—us. The argument was logical; it showed me my class heritage; the universal machine was working to perfection, and all this by relying on ideology. Somebody has said: "How absurd to destroy everything in order to realize the idea of justice!" For my part, I was trying to convince myself that in spite of everything, the aim was justice and that the price to pay could not be absurd.

Those were the thoughts going through my head in those days. During my various interrogations, even though the charges against me were absurd, I was helpless in the machinery. I was reasoning dialectically: "I am unjustly accused, but I am accused in the name of a just cause." I knew enough about history to have an idea of the inevitable cost of revolutions. At first, it was two officers who took turns putting questions to me. Then a woman who took over my case, a woman who was a political commissar, a zealot who before the war had been the heroine of a famous anti-Communist trial which ended in her being sentenced to life imprisonment. I suspected her of fighting for my soul. With blazing cheeks, she would try to explain to me that I was an objective enemy of the working class. I was neither their objective nor their subjective enemy. I tried to explain to her calmly that she was wrong, to show her the absurdity of the denunciation, and it was precisely my calmness that put her into a state. At other times the interrogation took the form of a great stir of ideas which I let myself be drawn into. These people had a small capacity for arguing. They did little more than repeat the same accusations *ad infinitum*: exploitation, oppression, poverty, police power. Before 1939 these watchwords were combated as subversive; now, with the support of the New Reality, they had acquired immense force. I could not hit upon the required answers, and I felt terribly ill at ease. Most of the time, they simply called me a reactionary and an agent of the Gestapo. There was

72

something lunatic and obsessive about it, as in the exorcisms of the Middle Ages. One of my interrogators, who sported a major's star on his tunic, had belonged to the Communist Party of western Belorussia before the war and had spent five years in a Polish prison. He muttered something to this effect as he thumbed through my file— it probably aroused in him nothing but heartfelt contempt—then he shot me a glance full of hatred, as if he wanted to spit in my face. I could see that, for people like him, imprisoning a man was a normal thing, no doubt because they themselves had been locked up. They had stewed in various prisons, Polish and Russian; it had been their internship, their apprenticeship and training camp. After a while, the whole thing comes to seem natural. First you find yourself under lock and key, then you send others there, and their faces get bashed in just as yours was. . . . When I wanted to know whether I was under arrest or not, the major shook his finger at me and told me that anybody who had not been in prison, in a hospital, and in army barracks knew nothing about life. For that brief instant, he seemed to me a man not devoid of good sense.

I was fully resigned. They demanded that I confess to the anti-Communist activities of "Rondo." I stubbornly denied without giving away a single name. It was of no use. Every time I went to one of these sessions, I was convinced I would not return. Yet I did, which is not to say that everybody returned. Certain fighters I had known in the Resistance died during these interrogations. One of them was locked up in a cell full of water. I shall never know why I escaped. Apparently, different methods were applied to each case, or—and this is the most likely supposition—no trace of "Rondo's" activities could be found. I must have seemed frivolous, and perhaps I deserved it.

But I want to stick to *your* questions, even though they cover such grandiose topics. . . . It is all quite confused. In the last analysis, the point is to recreate what I experienced during those years. But it is not at all easy, because I was living in confusion. All about me I saw oppression, fear, dreariness, and by the same token I was raking up all the conceivable arguments against myself, against my solitude and my anguish—as if I were sacrificing my comfort to pay a collective tribute. During our first conversation, you confided to me that those years of Polish life constituted for you a gap, that you had "missed" the psychological motives that animated a great many people at the time. You said, "I'm a few links short." And you were right. Many today are looking for the causes of their behavior and their way of thinking then, and they, too, lack certain links. Of those who kept quiet, some now realize that their silence was not entirely due to fear of the terror which was raging. They had proof enough during the war that they were not cowards. But theirs was not a moral protest either. Sometimes, years later, they ask themselves why they weren't able to do more. If they kept silent, was it not in the face of a reality that paralyzed the spirit? I think that they, too, experienced an inner split, often without being fully conscious of it. In 1956 theater directors and publishers were counting on the emergence of manuscripts full of revelations—plays, novels, poems written during the preceding years "for the bottom drawer." It turned out that the drawers were empty. At most, a dozen works of accusation came out, and only during the critical months when the shift came— some, indeed, afterward—as if no one had been sufficiently convinced of the merit of his views about those years, years which were still oppressing us. . . . The ideas and behavior of that period are being reconstructed today, after the event, and numerous theories explain one or another of our forms of activity or inactivity. Almost all are simplistic. Practically no one knows the truth. And the interpretations continue to cause cleavages, even though a quarter of a century has gone by and the true cleavages are different today. This makes me think of people who dig up aristocratic genealogies in a country where social ranks have long since been abolished.

During that time, I abandoned all hope. I felt of course that something justifiable was in progress, that irreversible transformations were taking place. Perhaps this is the way that one goes through revolutions. It seems as if faith in humanity were rooted in us more deeply than we think. When we learn of a terrible misfortune, when we come face to face with glaring injustice, our first reaction is to try to discover the cause, as if it were difficult to resign ourselves to accepting events devoid of all rational basis. . . . When someone reports a person's death, we would rather hear that he died from having gorged on an indigestible meal than that a mysterious tumor consumed his liver. Causes, causes . . . Once causes are in sight, everything can be clarified and reduced to effects. But certain events seem to me without rational cause. Thus in 1949 a man I had met in prison camp, after the Uprising, was condemned to death. Since he was one of the few officers of our former army to hold leftist beliefs, he had been accepted by the Polish army in 1945. Now, he was convicted for having taken part in a plot. I succeeded at the time in getting hold of someone who had also known him in prison camp and who might know more about his activities after the war. This influential person, who was in a position to get the information, assured me that the verdict rested on proof, and that the condemned man was said to have confessed. In such a case, you would suppose, one either believes or not, there is no third possibility. Yet there is one. I thought I detected in that whole story an element of oversimplification, too plain a way of solving the problem. Instead of closing my eyes (and believing) or opening them (and not believing), I made up my mind that he had apparently become involved in something "by accident." . . . When one reasons with vague ideas like "apparently," "by accident," and "something," it is difficult not to end up suspecting oneself, and one remains in an intermediate state between good faith and what one could call, for lack of a better word, self-deception. This is yet another of those symptoms of that *duality* I have already talked about. As it turned out, the solution *was* too plain. They stepped up the number of arbitrary arrests, they condemned innocent people; there were no reasons for the arrests, simply a goal—to frighten the population and to tighten up the ruling group. There is no bond quite like shedding other people's blood together. . . .

I lived through that period as in a mental illness that one hides. Every thought, practically, was double. Those in charge were simultaneously filling in the former gaps between social groups and tearing down the foundations of personal ethics. They were introducing free education, promoting political denunciation to the status of a duty. They managed to conquer illiteracy, and subjected the population to humiliating personal investigations. They popularized culture, but they put on it the corset of a rigid, monolithic doctrine. If I saw no reason to lament the fate of the industrialists or the expropriated nobles, I had good cause to deplore the news that reached us about the brutal treatment of the peasants who opposed the farm co-operatives.

Such a state of mental duality brings on symptoms comparable to those observable in clinical cases of depression. But, after a while, when that condition has become part of everyday life, the fundamental distinction between the normal and the pathological disappears. Perhaps it really was a mental illness. I know some people who claim to have gone mad at that time; and yet I lived, I talked, I brought up my daughter and I directed *Mrs. Warren's Profession* and *Maidens' Vows.*

With time, one manages to endure such a state of affairs like one's fate, like an aspect of life; one takes it to be a general feature of the age—or as still deeper, something belonging to the very essence of life. When I went to France for the first time in 1957 to attend a theater festival, and I saw in the airport at le Bourget a white sports car filled with tennis balls and golf clubs, I thought I had landed in a country of lunatics.

I spent three weeks in Paris. There I found many Polish friends from before the war, and fellow fighters from the Resistance. I spent a whole night walking on the Left Bank with a man who had been interrogated at the same time as myself by the Polish security forces, the UB, and by the same major. He called him a "ghastly brute." They had broken his fingers with a desk drawer because he had refused to sign an affidavit charging him with having handed Polish Communists over to the Germans. They slapped ten years' hard on him and he got out in 1955. Then he escaped to Sweden in a fishing boat. Today, he is one of the greatest anthropologists in the world. A charming man, he took part during the occupation in some military operations. A month ago in *Le Monde*, I came across his name under a protest by left-wing intellectuals. Certain phrases for the edification of the newspaper's readers seemed to come straight from the major's mouth: exploitation, oppression, police power. As for the major, he is now retired. I see him sometimes in

77

a little bar called The European, where I go for a cup of coffee when I have a free moment at the Institute. In summer I run into him in Ujazdowski Garden. We both like to feed the squirrels.

Do I consider myself a good man?

No, enough for today. That question is a killer. We'll go on tomorrow.

Chapter 6

It is nighttime. An hour ago the reception given at the Uld Raet Hoos after the final session of the convention was coming to an end. Come to think of it, perhaps it is not over yet, and I alone have had enough of it. Three hours of a bellowing crowd, glasses and plates in their hands, in old seventeenth-century rooms ... From the high ceilings, plump and smiling women tipped cornucopias over us while oxen watched us thoughtfully. I was the only one not wearing a dinner jacket, but just this morning I had bought a black bow tie to set off the gray of my lounge suit. By the grace of God, no one paid any attention to me. I thought again about your inquiry. Every evening, your questionnaire draws me irresistibly toward the hotel. I hurry like a drug addict who needs his little dose at a given hour. Yesterday, I reread the preliminary instructions. If this study is really going to consolidate the answers of three thousand persons coming from several dozen countries, I'm afraid my answers will exceed the admissible limits. I talk without being able to stop and I always have the feeling of not having said the most important things—there's an essential meaning or a leading thread that always eludes me. You know, during this reception tonight, when I was about to turn irreversibly into a sardine and was clearing a path toward the door, I suddenly saw in a small side-room a fairly husky man, wearing a gray suit, with a pipe in his mouth, and making his way toward me. Of course it was I who was walking toward a mirror. Such moments are in general rather painful—pointless encounters from which nothing can result, except perhaps a brief instant of bewilderment and sadness. When I saw myself in the mirror, I said to myself: Right! that's the fellow who talks every night in the hotel. And for a split second, I had the strange impression of being dissociated from my tapes, from this microphone and this box, which every evening swallows up a piece of myself. Then I immediately thought that if I reversed a tape to listen to it, it would be like the reflection in the mirror: a superfluous, somewhat sad encounter, a meeting with someone who is myself, but actually someone else, whom neither a mirror nor a tape can reflect. I stood there staring stupidly at myself while the crowd continued screaming as if in delirium, and, I—I don't know why—remembered my friend the dancer and his solo at the Poznan Opera, thirty-five years ago; those two taps with his heel, joyfully struck against the floor, with which he decided one evening to embellish his demonstration of czardas, and after which the public immediately rushed outside, the building having begun to rock on its base and the windows to shatter into bits. He kept on dancing, amazed at his own strength; for he did not know that the first two German bombs had fallen on Poznan.

Well, where was I?

Do you consider yourself a good man?

What, according to you, are the greatest dangers that threaten mankind today: overpopulation; the progress of technology; a cultural crisis; political theories; the collapse of ideologies? Delete as necessary.

If I put the two questions alongside each other, they seem to me to be very closely connected. I consider myself a man who *wants* to be good, and who, for that reason, finds himself threatened in that endeavor by two *great dangers*: history and nature. These, in my opinion, are the two main sources of trouble affecting personality. I think that man—and not only contemporary man—must confront them by submitting himself to constant self-control. I also think that the best, if not the only way, to effect this control is to keep an access route open to oneself. To put it another way, I am convinced that a man who wants to be good *can* defend himself against the pressures arising from the forces of nature and history. But he cannot defend himself effectively except by means of conscience. It is no accident that so many languages have only one word for psychological consciousness and moral conscience: *Conscience* . . . Naturally, what I want to talk about is a particular form of consciousness, centered on the subject, the consciousness of oneself. I cannot distinguish it from my moral conscience. If, on one of my bad days, I happen to feel a certain weariness with the world and with mankind, and if I quickly tell myself that it is only a projection of my weariness with myself, this counterattack is caused by my consciousness of self, which by the same token is none other than my moral conscience. And I would say that this identity is true at all times.

I've spoken of nature and of history and said that I found in them the main source of the troubles that can affect the personality. I belong to a certain type of contemporary man, a type particularly sensitized to history. To put it more precisely, *attentive* to History with a capital H. So far, nature has been indulgent to me: she has spared me enslavement to the body. I've not suffered from any serious illness, and I control my animal desires fairly easily. So I have no reason to complain. I am very fond of walking, the countryside, autumn, and films about dolphins. Between nature and me, a truce was struck long ago. I know the date. I have always been afraid of blind biological impulses, and it may be that which makes nationalism so alien to me; it contains a part of primitive bestiality. Besides, you must have noticed that I come from a different strain: I am much more strongly influenced by the rationalist tradition of social utopias than by any of the notions of tribal community that I was taught. That both alike involve the danger of mass extermination is something that I only slowly came to realize.

To be sure, people my age have lived very special lives. Our volcanos and our earthquakes have been historical above all. That is perhaps why the idea of history does not for us mean the past, but the moving force, ever changing, of the future. It is a sort of prophecy holding the present in bonds and fulfilling itself like a judicial sentence, which is accepted in advance, for it must be carried out willy-nilly. There is something shaming in those last two words; they express our acceptance of history as an external necessity. In fact, we create the necessity ourselves, by submitting to it before it becomes one. I have often noticed from observing a few friends who joined the Party during the 1950s that this surrender to a history coming from outside amounted to a sign of wisdom of the times. It seems a supra-personal spirit realizing itself independently of individual will and its morality. Its source is, I repeat, the future, unfathomable and unavoidable. In such a way does history replace ethics and faith and Providence.

It seems to me that the decisive moment hinges on an unconscious pact with necessity: "If it is bound to come anyhow, better join it." This is done to have a part in its fulfillment and also to conciliate it, to blunt its edge so that fewer heads will fall. This in turn means not merely to save one's own. But from the moment one concludes a pact with necessity, one must accept its reasons; and from then on, one must, from inside, like Jonah in the whale, justify these reasons oneself—talk in the voice of a whale and explain why it devours so many victims. As I said, there is no dearth of arguments, powerful arguments based on the logic of evolution and the foundations of justice. The sincere man who joined the Party stuck to one idea, to one program, though often with an unspoken reservation: "I accept everything except the methods." If after ten or twenty years it is precisely the "methods" that are challenged, his partial and unvoiced reservation rapidly invades his entire consciousness. He suddenly begins to speak another language without realizing that in the eyes of others he is one of those who have changed their opinion overnight. Suddenly, he comes out against the methods, convinced that he had always condemned them. True enough, he had condemned them in his thought. Now he condemns them out loud, he condemns necessity in its hour of weakness—a necessity at length corroded and compromised. He does not correct history until history has corrected itself. Reversals and re-positionings of this kind were frequent in 1956—all, without exception, following upon pacts once concluded with necessity.

Yes, indeed, there was an element of sinfulness in it; a collective sin whose effect was both secret and complicated, precisely because of the collective approval. Yet the heart of the problem is simple. It consists in what I called the projection, which is also the renunciation of oneself. As soon as I cease to be my own necessity to myself, I diminish reality in proportion by withdrawing myself from it, by withdrawing my will. I begin from that moment to submit to an impersonal abstraction which is indirectly of my own making and that of others like me —and others besides, not like me. The result: everyone becomes a tool of the anonymous machine he himself has built. I remember times when I felt that my behavior was in some strange way at once legitimate and unnatural. I am thinking in particular of an incident that took place in Wroclaw, in 1949, I think, when a writer gave me his new play to read. I was then the director of one of the theaters in the town. The play seemed interesting to me, but I thought: it will never get passed, it hasn't a prayer of passing. Whatever I might say to him, I was certain of one thing: no matter what, his play would not get passed. I told him that his play was not suitable for the stage. A little later, when I was having trouble getting to sleep, I realized that there were two levels of value, like two walls on which to hang a picture. Hung on one of them the picture seemed to me good, but when it was hung on the other, it became crude—indecently, provocatively crude. I had the feeling that those two levels were inside me and I was hanging the picture on both of them at once. But what it was actually worth I did not know because I did not know who I really was—because at such times we do not know who we are. I should like to find new words that might succeed in rendering the complexity of those moments—expressions like "planned integrity" and "delegated conscience." But it's only now, after the fact, that one tries to find such formulas. I had nothing left except my inner dilemma, a certain bitter taste—and yet inside I was beating the drums summoning all arguments to arms—probably the same arguments that had been used to convince me. One day, someone, I don't remember who, said to me: it may seem distant from you now, but for someone who has eaten his potatoes without salt—well, it's bound to come closer and closer. Do you call that an argument? I have only a lone and feeble consolation left from that theater incident. I advised the author to put his play in the bottom drawer; he should wait. For what? I do not know. I simply wanted to save him trouble. I believe I added that we were living in the age of the dictatorship of the proletariat. Not a word more. But my "no matter what, it will not get passed," implied something more. Unconsciously, I wanted to be in tune with my times, with the period. That does not necessarily mean in harmony with oneself. And such is my opinion today.

I spoke about the past. Today things are simpler, more commonplace, as if someone had changed them into smaller print. It's certainly less dangerous that way. All in all, I do not consider myself worn down. Perhaps I owe this to the fact that I did not draw all the conclusions from the premises of history. I have not been able, it is true, to entertain the possibility of my own destruction through a just cause, but luckily I was not astute enough to think that a just cause could swallow up a million people. Besides, I am not altogether sure that I have always been safe. I was on holiday in the mountains when I heard the announcement on the radio of the death of a man who for many years symbolized dialectic providence. He had hardening of the arteries, and it seems he died shaking his fist at someone. A poet—one of his victims—had called him "the solitary man-eater." Three years later, during a conference at the university, my friend Icz opened his speech with these words—"Not only had the Emperor no clothes, he was a statue built with newspapers!"

There was an enormous crowd at that conference; everybody had come, that is to say, two thousand people of

85

all persuasions whose positions and life stories had worked out in different ways—both before and after. On the crest of this wave, Icz had emerged—pale, reactivated, with his prominent Adam's apple and shrill voice. In the preceding years he had belonged to the group of sympathizers whom editors could rely upon. He had published reviews and articles, sharply critical, skillfully disposed. For example, he blamed the prewar literature for being egocentric and found in it the legacy of the petit-bourgeois mentality. But he did this from the point of view of the nineteenth-century classics of realism (his essay, "Balzac, a Lesson in Anatomy," caused quite a stir in its time). What struck me most in his argument was that he did not go after the truly dangerous individuals. He attacked those whom he had blamed a few years previously for lagging behind reality and for moving away from the realistic tradition of enlightenment and positivism. Now, he accused them of having betrayed themselves, "it so happened"—to them. I suppose that the power of his speech derived from his knowledge of the subject: Icz was talking about himself and attacking himself. It was an inspired self-denunciation, probably spontaneous and perhaps even disinterested, but above all penetrating. He knew his weaknesses, and in analyzing them through the example of others, he shed light on their threatening characteristics. That made him one of the heroes of the day. But I knew him well, and he did not convince me. The next day, when he telephoned, we made a date for coffee at the Bristol. Icz arrived late, he had another date at the club for young intellectuals. He asked me right away what I thought of his speech. I told him that he had spoken remarkably well, and that he had been applauded by, among others, a goodly number of sons-of-bitches, i.e., by those he had spared. I added that there was one thing I did not understand: why he had attacked people who were the least dangerous, people who, as he must know, had *never exterminated anybody*, nor tried to suppress anyone. Why them, and not the others? And I repeated, "The sons-of-bitches." I wanted to add: "You did it because you're still afraid of them and you know they will never change." But I resisted the impulse, and do you know what he answered? He said: "You don't understand; this is revolution." Then he started to explain that every revolution has its victims, and I felt sure that the next minute he would be telling me about the bulldozers of history. I was filled with rage. My only thought was, "Oh, you idiot, you idiot with ideas instead of a mind!"— and I missed my chance to blow up: he was in a hurry, he had another appointment.

Then I did something rather difficult to explain: I filled out an application to join the Party. No doubt it was a gesture inspired by irritation, or perhaps by the desire to emphasize my independence: a somewhat ridiculous gesture, in that I injected into it the meaning of an autonomous act in the midst of a collective catharsis. At that time, everybody, all together, were repudiating in chorus fashion not only his own but other people's ideas. Quite often, one would cut off part of one's biography. All this was done in public, in front of an overheated audience, in an atmosphere halfway between oratorical eloquence and moral exaltation, in which the most diverse interests and designs mix and mingle inextricably. But the primary, fundamental motive lay in the very heart of the nation—that was clear to everybody. What a pity you did not visit Poland during that period! You would have seen a strange country, where the cities seemed taken over by the young while the big shots were being carted out of factories in wheelbarrows. The press had revived, clubs and student cabarets began to spread, political prisoners were let out again. The crowd chased the old ideologists off the rostrum like so many chickens; it was the workers and the artists who held the floor during meetings. When we refer to that period—it lasted barely two years—we simply say *October*. During the third year, the clubs began to be closed down, the press throttled. By the fourth, it was over: broken, crushed. It was over and everybody knew there was no further hope of freedom. But that was something we could not foretell during the first two years, and my gesture was then nothing more than a bizarre, almost irrational act—I did it, no doubt, to push against the dialectic evolution propounded by Icz, if not to push against myself; or to be exact, against a part of myself. Indeed, it seems that I have always been in a state of internal contradiction, due to this impaired vision of mine which makes the present—or I should say, the public present, the present of words and deeds—look like a manly, compulsory game between man and necessity, a game in which one must take part if one wants really to live. In any case, my application remained fruitless. It was accepted and then nothing happened, as if it had fallen into oblivion—no request for an interview. The piece of paper must have wound up in a drawer, and I think that is the best thing that could have happened to it.

In hopes of making it easier for me to answer the question which concerns us now, the questionnaire lists in parentheses a few of today's realities, pointing out how each represents a particular danger for man: *the primacy of technology, overpopulation, crises in culture and in the ideologies* . . . If I fail to speak of them, it is because they are evolutionary in character, they belong with those events that spring from evolution. Either evolution overtakes such events, or they are events that fulfill the evolutionary cycle, and then we have a civilization on its way out. If I say nothing about these occurrences, then, it is not that they are unimportant, but that in my answers I am above all concentrating on myself. Am I being clear-minded? Not about the world and civilization, but about the way I must live and think, about what threatens me and what I want or don't want. I think that the dangers that threaten me personally have always threatened man and will continue to threaten him, notwithstanding the phases of evolution. In talking about these dangers I feel that I am broaching eternal themes. I am not convinced that the first steps of man on the moon will in future free people like myself from destinies like mine; nor do I believe that any future evolution is capable of ridding us of the most profound human uncertainty—the distinction between Good and Evil in any given situation. If, therefore, I have correctly defined the two greatest dangers that threaten man, it is because I consider them my own, truly personal; and it is with the most thorough conviction that I can claim to fear nothing worse than History above me and Nature within me. With less pathos, let me say: I fear nothing more than the loss of access to myself. I mean access to myself when attacked by this fake, double "self" engendered by an unchecked biology and a satanic future. "The moral law within me" is nothing more than a formula to delineate the boundaries of human liberty. Whatever answer I give to whatever question, I must infallibly return to this formula, because in the end, it is the one on which rest the foundations of humanity. All thoughts lead to and proceed from there: whether the question relates to politics or art, it will always involve the moral will and whatever, with its help, we can make of ourselves.

But one must decide: Does one view the moral law in

man as the *transmission* of man's social experience or as a *commandment* emanating from sources older and deeper than human experience? In other words, the question missing from the study should go like this: *According to you, what is the origin of ethics? Is it social or metaphysical?* I cannot readily imagine a man who does not ask himself that question. If I do not want to kill, I want to know why I do not want to kill, and I want to explain to myself how I come by the certainty that killing is forbidden. To explain to myself the certainty . . . that may be asking too much. Let us rather say: find again this conviction within myself. Is morality a convention one can modify, or an imperative immutable in its essence? That is one of the most widely discussed philosophical questions, but also one of the most important and most personal one can ask. I would strongly urge you to include it in your study.

My answer? My answer derives from my ignorance. Not knowing what the Beginning is, I must regard it as an unknown quantity. Not knowing what the End is, either, I must regard what exists between the two as an unknown also. Not knowing what causes movement inside the atom, I must regard the energy of organic matter as one of the mysteries of life. The cause of my self and its meaning are equally inaccessible to me. Yet in the mythology of every culture one finds the same symbols indicating a link between the essence of life and the value of virtue, as well as the trinity of cause, means, and end. These symbols generally link the will of God to the fate of man, with his merits and his faults, with a reward or a punishment. And this is true not only in our white, Graeco-Judaeo-Christian culture. The religious ontologies of the East have ethical roots, too; man's actions are judged in a transcendental light, and souls after death have to

90

complete a voyage which will lead them to eternal harmony. These common symbols seem to suggest that what we call Evil is an irregularity, a deviation from a path with which we are unfamiliar. So all things considered, being a responsible man, I should stop at the borderline which marks the sphere of my ignorance, then reflect and, as I said, decide. But decide what? Decide to adopt a working hypothesis which clashes with neither logic nor instinct. I suffer my ignorance and my fear of evil in silence. Without seeking to elucidate the mystery of life, without giving it a name—as previously prescribed—I distrust evil because I am aware of its possible evil consequences, here below and in other worlds unknown to me. This attitude conforms better to reason than the rationalist certainty, which is limited by the senses. One of my friends, a theoretical physicist, explained to me one day what his research work on the structure of the atomic nucleus consisted in: You must, he said, imagine a Ping-Pong ball thrown into a completely dark room. You are then supposed to discover the position of the walls and the furniture from the information transmitted by the echoes and the rhythm of the bouncing ball. I said that I wanted to be a good man—let us look at it as a kind of an experiment in a dark room. I would have to choose a certain type of behavior in there. I choose the simplest: to behave, in relation to others and to oneself as well, as if there was light in the room and as if our Judge had come to take his seat; to act and to think, that is to say, as if God existed and as if evil could be entirely rooted out. I consider this working theory as the most salutary. But if I embrace this simple hypothesis, formerly used in the rearing of children, I must build it on the ground of my personal experience, including the knowledge I have of the world—which is far from simple and in no way childish. No, it is not easy. But, I repeat, all this is a proposal one makes to oneself and for one's benefit.

I expect that the authors of the questionnaire would like to know how I introduce this hypothesis into my daily life. Without going into details, I can assert at least one thing: the first condition is to reduce one's wants. On this point our opinions are going to differ. In the West today you identify, on the one hand, the development of the individual with the ever-greater satisfaction of whims and wants; and, on the other, you join together freedom and the right to happiness. But my hemisphere of consciousness reacts differently. It is possible that its reactions are amputated by a cycle of history in which the needs of an individual could not fully emerge, blocked by an outside force or a collective self-induced impotence. In societies where slavery is perceived as the effect of fate imposed from the outside, freedom becomes a religious concept, something that one longs for, something that has to come from outside, from fate, and not from a human right. Freedom so conceived is not a social attribute of man but is a salvation. The right to happiness doesn't exist in this concept of freedom, though dying for it is real enough. Thus, for me to reduce my needs is certainly easier than for someone brought up to expect a happy life in California. It is all the easier for me because, as I have said, I've managed for quite a while to control my instincts without much difficulty. What is more, I think— and here, too, we will undoubtedly differ—that freedom consists in controlling and curbing one's instincts and not in satisfying them. If I do not check it within myself, nature increases my dependence and enslavement. For example, in satisfying the instinct of ownership, I imprison myself in a web of constraint and dependency; whereas by reducing my needs I escape from the system and I become much more difficult to catch. That amounts to saying that I own more in having less, because I retain the ownership of what is authentic about myself. In short, we differ on many points, but that, too, is one of the objects of your inquiry.

THIS YEAR I came back from vacation at the end of August. My daughter had spent the last week with me. We and a group of other passengers were waiting late in the evening for the Warsaw train. It didn't seem to be coming. The time in the schedule had long since gone by, but we had been given no word about the length of the delay. It was cool. About twenty people with children and suitcases were freezing, standing up or sitting on the benches, while I was trying to cut the wait by walking back and forth along the platform, between the sign showing the name of the station and the station clock. After half an hour, Mewa came up to me to ask if I hadn't had enough walking. She was outraged at the way we were being treated. I shrugged my shoulders. The train would come eventually, and I went back to my walk. I saw from a distance that Mewa was in conversation with a group of people; she was gesticulating, with a cigarette in her hand, and by the time I came around to the clock, she had disappeared from the platform. I found her in the control room where an employee with a cap on his head was drinking his tea. She was demanding that he give her the complaint book. By sheer persistence, she forced him to telephone the main station. When we went out on the platform, the loudspeaker announced that the train was expected at a certain time, at which Mewa began to laugh and I once again shrugged my shoulders. I resumed my sauntering toward the clock. By then it was past eleven. A starlit August night; I think there were some crickets somewhere.

The travelers were still sitting on the benches. A child began to cry. Leaning against a post, Mewa tried to read the book she had brought with her. When the train finally arrived, the people hurled themselves into the coaches, which were already packed with people. We finally managed to get a seat, but only at the last minute. And that is not the point of the story. I could have paced up and down the platform for an hour or two more without its ever occurring to me to assert my rights. What did I think about as I walked? What does one usually think about when waiting for a train? Well, that it's cold and that one has been waiting a long time. Once, in 1945, I waited three days in more than twenty degrees below zero for the train from Zabkowice to Warsaw. Now, at least, I had a warm coat and a pipe. What is more, I knew that there was a schedule and that sooner or later we would get on. Right now, I could not possibly plumb the depths of my mind; I can only recapture the mood I was in, and that mood assuredly had nothing to do with the field of social rights. Rather, there was something in it akin to the relation of a peasant to nature: I was waiting for the train just as, in summer, one waits in the country for the rain. If I was demanding anything it was of myself alone—for outward control, peace, patience. It was a kind of confirmation of my beliefs about the imponderable nature of events. I gave no thought to my rights; I did not believe in rights. That train, those three freezing nights at Zabkowice, must have left their mark on me. I was waiting with the others, now as then, feeling neither cheated nor humiliated, never thinking that it might be possible to change or demand anything, wishing only to preserve my personal dignity and a kind of honor in the face of darkness and the void. Everybody, probably, those waiting as well as the stationmaster drinking his tea, felt as if cut off from

94

freedom; we were waiting motionless, as if our moorings had come loose, hoping for something to loom out of the shadows. But, if you stop to think of it, we were in the realm of the absurd, in unreality—all of us, except my daughter who believed in rights. Yet one thing she didn't notice: the look the stationmaster gave me when I came into the smoky room. True, I could have been someone who travels incognito with a young and pretty woman, someone who for once is not using his company car. That stationmaster, who must know the power of fate, came to life when he saw my briefcase. At any rate that is what I surmised, but I did not let on. Now, it seems to me that my daughter and I embodied two different ideas of liberty; the stationmaster, on the other hand, had the reaction of a slave.

I am going to bed. See you tomorrow.

ONE MORE WORD, after taking a shower. In my working theory, if you remember, in what I call an experiment in the black chamber, I suspect there is an element of utopianism, an abstract principle impossible to satisfy in practice, because life . . . It's easy to complete that sentence. Life—a trite explanation and yet it has cut deep into human consciousness. With us it has become the most familiar commonplace.

In our everyday speech the word *utopia* has taken on an ironic connotation. It allows us to reject with a clear conscience any thirst for the ideal, any faith in the Good or in Reason. What is wanted is to sober up the popular mind, bring it back to reality. To cry "Utopia!" is to decline to take flight; it is a shrug of the shoulders to remind others of all abortive movements; it is the final gesture of someone whose wings have been clipped. Everybody's wings have been clipped and it is too late to fly. In college slang, when referring to an older woman, they say in a blasé tone of voice "a courier in the Resistance." Our language is now full of expressions like that. Obviously you are not familiar with them. These metaphors are all of the same sort, cut from the same cloth, from the same distrust of values. But the business is not so simple as it appears, because there is at the same time a kind of thirst for meaning, a yearning for ideas. And this can be proved, if only by our passion for art. We never make fun of art. The language of politicians is made up of stock phrases: we don't believe them, even when they extol first-aid for the drowned. We do not believe in words. Words are reproducible. Modern-day hell is paved with words. Words supply information; but values, essence, spirit, one expects to obtain those from art. Today the biographies of artists are like the lives of the saints, their works are like relics, they are priceless. And if that is true, it is no doubt because artists have survived the chaos of the times without abandoning their Ten Commandments and have taken disinterested risks. Through their opposition to reality and their posthumous glory, they have shown that virtue paid. You know, even the juvenile delinquents have a sort of dour respect for art.

All of this sounds grand. One might wonder why I speak of it. To comfort myself, of course. To remember. Not to lose my head and not to be thrown back into the void. I say "utopia," "utopian." Social utopias form the framework of our culture and indicate the path it must take. And yet, is there not in all cultures a need to realize religion and achieve it right here, on earth? Undoubtedly you know that the Inca—or Aztec—priests had determined very precisely the year and month when their liberating god would come to the earth and that it was in that very year and month that strange huge ships landed on their shores and creatures with pale faces disembarked, led by a plumed angel in golden armor. The Aztecs threw themselves at his feet before he cut their throats. The harbinger of death, the angel of massacre was Cortez, as you know. But you can guess that I haven't—in fact, haven't had for some time—such a strong need for contact with gods of earthly extraction, and you are right. As I told you, I do not believe in any rites, religious or political. I could add that I expect nothing. As for the visitation of cohorts in armor, I have already lived through it. Sometimes I worry: what's left of me in the end? I detest despair and nothingness. I should like to die in peace. To inhabit the absurd and to persist in living—there is something low and mean about that, for with one motion one could be done with it. That's why I reply: I want to go on living—*as if* there were a meaning to it; *as if* I knew the reason and the purpose and I could survive my own death; *as if . . . As if* the world were governed by a Good which God had bestowed on man. In your questionnaire you ask: *What is your definition of man?* I haven't a definition of man, but if I had I would say: the creature that gives a meaning to existence.

Chapter 7

AFTER OUR telephone conversation earlier today, I still wanted us to meet. You know how it is: one regrets one's initial reaction—accidental, careless words, sometimes the wrong tone of voice. It may come from being unprepared or from embarrassment or from a completely silly reason: one is in bed or in the bath. It doesn't matter where I was when the telephone rang: it is nevertheless true that, having hung up, I wanted to dial your number. Or rather, to cancel my reaction—and, as you had suggested, make an appointment to meet. But, in the first place, I could not think of your number, I would have had to look it up in my little book; and then, a minute later, I realized that my refusal had not been accidental.

I am afraid that if we met it would make it more difficult for me to continue these tapes. Perhaps I would even get nervous about the ones I have already done. Perhaps I would want to listen to them again. But then I would be listening to them with you beside me, and imagining your reactions. It would be like writing a letter to someone who is nearby and is reading over your shoulder. It borders on the ridiculous.

That is why I gave up the idea of meeting.

I return to your questions. Your questionnaire includes several items concerning my family status, my entourage, my standard of living, and my income. Number seventeen is about [*my*] *wife's profession*; number eighteen is about *the make of* [*my*] *car*. The most interesting are the subsidiary points designated by letters. They are more precise and therefore disclose the true aim of the survey. I am asked to specify *the make of my present car, the make of the last one*, and *the make of the one which I expect to buy*. The point is obvious: it is to classify me in the right social class, the makes of my successive cars representing so many rungs on the climb up the social ladder. But here the study draws a complete blank and betrays a poor knowledge of the conditions that obtain in my country. You see, what the make of my car is is a question that makes me laugh. In Wroclaw, I drove in an official car for a month; it was a Pobieda, with a chauffeur who took a very professional interest in my daily life. Since then, I have never "changed" anything except buses. On the other hand, my son-in-law has had for a year a savings book for a car purchase stamped PKO, which means—I'd rather not go on with the question; I could do it only by giving an explanation of all the differences between life-styles in our two hemispheres. And during our first conversation you warned me to avoid that line of thought.

I am myself trying to avoid a useless piling up of autobiographical details, not because they are too personal but because it would not interest me to recount them. In what I want to say, it is the conclusions that interest me the most. I know my life-story by heart, and what I can remember does not matter to me. What does matter to me is what I know least and what I am least sure about. You could compare me to a man who remembers exactly what goods he has bought and sold but who doesn't know his bank balance. If, for example, I answer the question about my attitude toward the institution of marriage, I find the question a good one, because it forces me to frame an answer I do not yet know and which will therefore define me at the very moment that I give it—and much better than would a reply to a question about my marriage, because *that* answer I know even before the question is put. Any answers we know by heart become less and less genuine with time, moving, as they do, further and further away from the original truth all the time. I should like to extract from myself this self with whom I live every day, with whom I eat and walk and sleep, and learn whether he in fact knows how to think, or if he has only grown by the amount of his footsteps and his sleep.

So, for the time being, I will skip the question of marriage and, to stay within the range of motors, I will go on to another question: *What is the main moving force in your behavior? Would you call it social, moral, biological, or what?* This sort of thing leads me straight into fiction. The principal force—social, moral, biological? Am I to cross out what doesn't apply? One can find the motor in a Ford Cortina, but in *me*? The question is badly worded. Let us begin with the fact that a normal man does not in general know the real reasons for his behavior. Sometimes, of course, he does succeed in grasping them—sometimes, but not always. That is called self-awareness. In the light of outbursts and inner cracks one discovers that one's self is by itself several people, busy deceiving and arguing with each other; that one possesses contradictory opinions about oneself and that one can interpret one's conduct in different ways. It appears that one knew almost nothing about oneself the day when, for example, one first killed a man. Let us suppose, for instance, that this man is a rival in love. The instinct which impels to killing a rival is a biological urge: one male killing another. In the world of men, there is a law that forbids killing. And in this case, it turns out that the rival is a danger to the community. He could, by his acts, cause the death of worthy people. The moral principle therefore bends under social pressure; the murder is justified in the interests of the public welfare. In such a case, the murder is a resultant of several forces. To go on, let us suppose further that the man who fires the weapon is not aware of this construct—which I sketch here in broad outline. To him the motives for his act will seem simple, though they are in fact the product of the milieu in which he lives. Such acts the milieu calls *duty accomplished*—in our particular case, the duty of a patriot, citizen, or soldier. Such is the consciousness which the doer has of his deed: a collective *conscience* has replaced his personal conscience. Let us go on one more step. Let us imagine that, several years later, our hero learns that the man he has killed from duty had been far more intimate with a certain woman than she wished at the time to admit. His act thereby loses its simple and obvious dimension; in a second he is questioning his motives for the murder: could it have been unconscious jealousy? Then other notions, other possibilities, other insights take shape in his mind, new conjectures, mixed and superimposed on each other. The feelings of years past come back to life and fill his thought, which continues to struggle and go around in a circle, which comes up against the same intricate web of pressures and conflicts. But by now, his nature has ceased to be simply a part of the collective conscience; it wants to examine itself, to take note of its components and of the laws that determined it. In the end, if one can speak of any end, my imaginary hero will not know the "main moving force" of his conduct. At best, he will conclude that the reasons impelling him were manifold, that they were in conflict and, at the same time, that they supported each other. Perhaps, if he lacks courage in self-analysis, he will eventually deceive himself, and think that he killed his enemy solely from concern for the general welfare. But if he does not shrink back, if he does want to pursue the investigation of himself, he will only get doubts for his pains. He will feel that he has not succeeded in identifying himself and in isolating his own ultimate truth. He will only have reached the place where what is not truth becomes visible. From then on, it is from that vantage that he will observe himself and he will never be able to leave it. That is what one might call the main moving force of his behavior.

In this description, only the moment of shock, a few years afterward, is genuine. And yet we have only to change the facts a very little for everything to be as I reported it to you. If, instead of sneaking the pistol away from me, she had forewarned me, and if I had decided to get rid of him myself, I would have learned, three years later, that I had killed a man with whom she was involved. I remember being staggered when she told me, "It was I who shot him, at night, on his sofa." And my reply was: "How lucky you never told me at the time." I felt pretty much like a man who hears a time bomb explode in a room he has just left. We were in Wroclaw, in the spring of 1948, on the eve of our divorce. For an instant, I thanked God for having sent me the truth with several years' delay. If three years earlier, in March 1945, I would never have gone to Kielce and brought my daughter back with me.

That's that. Now here is the twentieth question: *How important a role does sexual drive play in your life? What personal problems derive from it?*

I choose this question now in order to relax. I have

already said several times that without much trouble I manage to keep a tight rein on the instincts of the body, and this not solely because of a rigorous character. Imagine a young man whose sexual urge developed early. He is sufficiently sensitive to feel ashamed and guilty about these arousals: he finds them humiliating. The sight of a woman's leg is enough to make him fantasize. Each new girl he meets becomes an object of desire. At every encounter, in a movie theater or out walking, he is obsessed with a single idea: if, when, and how he will possess this or that woman. He is in a state of permanent tension, consumed by a desire he must hide and which lowers him in his self-esteem. Because he always looks at himself from the outside, with the smiling face of a Don Juan full of false promises, he sees himself as a caricature of himself and he is prey to unbearable doubts after each conquest. He is convinced that he does not know how to love. As soon as his attempts are crowned with success, he feels distaste for his partners. He feels in all this an emotional vacuum, a sort of vile lowering which makes a slave of him. He knows he lies and uses tricks, he wrecks his idea of human relationships in which, on the far side of his obsession, love, friendship, and faithfulness must exist. He knows this but he is powerless. He suspects that he is dealing with forces that he cannot change and that he will not resist. But in the end, this great flaw does not prevent him from living, passing his exams, going on vacation.

One year, during a holiday spent in Polesie with the relatives of a school friend, I fell off a horse. My shoulder was wrenched by a root, but, despite the pain, I picked myself up without help. The accident took place on the outskirts of a wood. I got back by teatime, reeling, but not breathing a word of the accident to anyone. After dinner I had an appointment with my friend's cousin, a young married woman who was not putting obstacles in my way. Our walk was to end in a shed: a roomy landau without doors or seats was garaged there. We spent three hours there that night, and for the first time in my life I talked with a woman without wanting to have her down on the floor, even though that was her expectation. To tell the truth, it was also mine. It could have happened; I even think it should have. I merely thought that the predictable end now looked less important; I kept delaying as if already, in advance, I would be missing the quiet pleasure of the conversation, which should have given way to rhythmic panting and spasms. We talked until midnight, about her husband (whom she undoubtedly loved) and about unfaithfulness in marriage (did it mean the same thing for a man as for a woman?). She was intelligent. Later I met many intelligent and attractive women with whom I enjoyed talking. During the years that followed, I experienced a few intimate relationships and love. If you are still puzzled, I can tell you in so many words: that fall from a horse had completely changed me. It is somehow incredible. The change came about in a mechanical way; when I got up from the ground I was already a different man. X rays showed only the slightest displacement of some vertebrae, and it is as if thanks to that I had regained my human dignity. The thing happened from one day to the next, or more exactly in half an hour. If I had come out of the accident a cripple for life, the thing would be easier to understand. But to become a decent fellow as the result of a bump, that's no joke. It is as if all of a sudden I was freed from all that was uncivilized in me, as if my conscience had been awakened. Just think of it! The awakening of a conscience through the slipping of some vertebrae! From that time on I was able to be "fair" and not deceive my female partners. I learned how to curb my instincts and control my reactions. I became capable of greater calm, of showing myself disinterested, and I grew immune to jealousy insofar as it is biological in origin. But was this transformation quite normal? Is it quite normal that the slipping of some vertebrae should have spared me the arduous conquest of salvation? What would have happened if I had not fallen off my horse? Sex maniacs are not always horsemen. What must those do who have never fallen off? Upon my word, I don't know. Good night.

BETTER AND BETTER. Yesterday I got back to my hotel at dawn; today, I begin the day with my mind a blank. I have just listened to the final sentences on the tape in order to carry on my solo. Where was I? At the point where fifteen hundred years ago the minds of the Church fathers were certainly kept busy. The builders of the Christian world were intellectuals. The Church was born of debates. The pillars of the faith, its ideas and its means of action are the result of polemics and correspondence. Their authors were people aware of the laws of psychology, men who possessed a profound knowledge of life. They must have made up a list of questions: What should man do with his instincts, with his desires and his fears? How can his need for freedom be channeled? How can his slavery be hidden from him? What is he to do with his awareness of death? What ought he to receive in exchange for his ignorance of causes and of ends? And so on—a very long questionnaire. The fathers of Christianity worked for centuries in order to answer these questions. The time you've allowed me is more limited. Well then, what must people do who haven't fallen off a horse, the lost souls, those who are slaves to their blood or their sperm? And what must they do whom nature has condemned to other infernal sufferings? You see, I don't think I have the mind for moral philosophy. But this question is as concrete as they come, it deals with practical problems. The fathers of Christianity practiced just this sort of realism; they knew the ways of the world. They thought that one could earn salvation by working hard for it. They gave you a chance, a recourse. Perceptive moralists do not construct cells without windows or cages from which one can't escape. Salvation depends upon effort. It does not demand trial by fire. It banks on suffering and hope. It asserts that suffering is necessary but advises against despair. And above all, it maintains that it is never too late, not for anyone. As for the rest, salvation is a private affair; heaven turns its glance away from the relation between individuals and power. Render unto Caesar that which is Caesar's—does that not imply that heaven takes into account the dilemma of honest people condemned to live under tyrants? Heaven thereby leads to the prayer stool, not to the scaffold. For the Christian theologians were mindful of the multiplicity of experiences and recognized the limits of human resistance to nature and to history. But they must have been profoundly convinced of one thing: that truth is only found beyond the visible world and that it cannot be brought closer to man except by attaching a meaning to his life and to his death.

You know, I don't think it will be easy to give any better answer than this. It is well thought out, geared to the average man, while it also raises that average. It enhances him through perplexity, meditation, and the consciousness of what his liberty is, as well as by postulating a universal principle. It was all intelligently conceived in relation to mankind. Even before my fall from the horse I wasn't a declared candidate for hell. Deep down inside, I did not think that man was bad and I managed to see in the world something superior to material values. If that horse had not thrown me, I would have had to keep on stewing in my own juice and living like others. But to live with contempt for myself, that was no doubt beyond me—which was already a point in my favor. It meant that I expected something from myself, that I was trying to change myself in some way, and that I was in torment. An old actor with whom I used to play billiards before the war, in the café next to the theater, used to say that actors are divided into three categories: the bad, the good, and the great. The great actors are the good ones who improve. And I believe in progress. I am convinced that everyone has his chance, and that it is never too late for anyone. Is it really impossible to force ourselves to be more human? After all, what else do we do other than strive to increase our humanity? The results are more or less good, results—more or less; sometimes less than more.

I have strayed from your questions. Blame it on last night. Two young actors from Studio XX took me thirty kilometers outside the city in their Volkswagen. I spent the night in an old mill, a mill which houses a sort of artistico-religious sect for the young. It may even be a political movement or a group of drug addicts. I don't know; it was difficult for me to figure it out. The boys had hair down to their shoulders and wore tunics or dresses enlivened with necklaces. The girls, with their small childlike breasts, were in pants and torn sweaters. They took a liking to me; for them I was undoubtedly a sort of Professor of Revolutions. They knew that the Communists were in power in Poland and this is how it happened that a bespectacled Christ wearing a German iron cross around his neck asked me questions about Rosa Luxemburg and about our youth. He wanted to know whether her writings were being studied.

We sat on mattresses, listening to Beethoven and Haydn. Next to me, a young girl whose shoulder was embellished with a phallic tattoo whispered to me that she was a Maoist-Trotskyite-Guevarist and that her name was Uth Seenzen. Afterward, I sniffed and smoked something, but to no effect. Then I leaped about with everybody else while beating a drum. I seem to recall that it was an African drum with hairs and tails. Uth Seenzen—a very pretty name. She is five years younger than my daughter. She called me by my first name. I felt rather as if I were playing the part of a socialist Santa Claus or that of Mr. Pickwick dreaming about goblins. No matter. I had resolved to let nothing surprise me, and that did not work too badly. Right up to the end I played my part, even in the darkness, sitting on my tom-tom. The others politely let me be with my pipe. I was sitting in a cloud of incense, presumably Indian. From the darkness I could hear whisperings and cries. Later on, when the young girl came back, we got into a discussion. What about? Taxes. I learned that they were fighting against the tax benefits for the elderly. A new system of insurance had just been set up to make life easier for those over sixty years old. Society takes care of you, the government supplies an apartment with a free telephone, simply to enable you to get hold of a doctor. You must have heard of it. And behold, Uth Seenzen and her friends now organize street demonstrations in protest! They won't pay taxes to provide for other people's old age, because they want for themselves a short life and a violent death! They commit suicide, they kill themselves on the highways, old age will never reach them.

After a while the girl left; somebody had taken her into the dark. I wanted to laugh, because I saw myself in the ruins of a mill, at night, sitting on the tom-tom of a black warrior, while all around me a dozen couples were making love to the sound of Beethoven's Fifth. What a far cry from the moral-sexual problems of my youth! Uth Seenzen would have been astounded at the notion that anyone could link sex with ethics. Her youth is emancipated from prudishness and deceit; the pill has cleared the road of any pitfalls. Such is this new, wonderful world where children have as much right to sensual pleasure as they have to food and drink and shelter—a world from which old age has disappeared. And still I felt like laughing. I did not altogether believe in this new, wonderful world and this liberated youth. I sensed a hint of deceit in that incense and those drums. And in those cries and costumes, in that mixture of revolution and modishness. A different deceit, of course, from the one I know and in which I live. It operates in another way, certainly more colorful and less organized . . . And so they are idealists, they have original minds and freedom like the birds; they wear chasubles, stoles, and surplices; they've adopted the life-style of artists, the philosophers' contempt for a profession, and the revolutionists' contempt for the past. But they have produced no religion, no art, no philosophy, no revolution. Perhaps they constitute a mere masquerade during one of history's intermissions.

I was drowsing on this drum, but from time to time, I would wonder which of the two, them or me, was the more humanly genuine in our present world. Me, a friendly old Slav with my historico-dialectic biography brim-full of *Polishness*—or them, with their youth and their union of bodies, rhythmic with slogans, sex, and stereo. They with their gurus or I with my *Warsaw Life*. I then felt less inclined to laugh; I felt pity—for them and no doubt for myself as well. Perhaps the music had upset me a little, but nevertheless I was on to something. I was beginning, in the darkness, to be seized by a thought, a simple thought—the thought of death, which both for them and for me would come alike; death, which is the most genuine thing there is, which one cannot cheat or hide from. I was obviously delirious, you will say. Possibly, but now I am lucid.

In your questionnaire there is no question about death. The subject has been scrupulously avoided. God, freedom, cars, the family, education—well and good. The survey wants answers on almost every subject—except that one. It is Americans who made up the questions and that explains a lot. Americans do not like to talk about death; you must have noticed it. Civilization and death—not a very cheering contrast. Young civilizations, making great strides, are fundamentally optimistic; the fact of dying seems to them like one of nature's mistakes, a technical imperfection. Moreover, this imperfection will be removed in the new, wonderful world to come. There are many different conceptions of this new world, but whether it be a classless or a postindustrial society, conjuring up the skeleton is nowhere looked upon favorably. In this wonderful new world, Uth Seenzen dies quickly and early; death must be as unnoticeable as an injection during sleep. You see, they, too, are children of civilization. Or possibly little children lost. They are heirs to machinery and the science lab, and their revolt is an inverted faith in life. That is one of the characteristics of civilization. Culture is interested in death, but civilization must believe in life. Am I boring you? I'm afraid that I am repeating things that have long since been said. You must

111

be thinking that only a terribly gloomy fellow would associate the sight of a handsome wench with death. But perhaps not so gloomy as he seems and—who knows, what other association of ideas might occur to this fellow?

A man who has passed the fifty-year mark is like a gazelle—one look from a girl can kill him. We must take precautions against such hunters; we are not so numerous that we can afford to run around the landscape as we please. And as for her, what could she figure out about me? As it turned out, she quietly withdrew. I, too, used to run away; tales in which the hero was over twenty-five years old would bore me. It is not until later that such thoughts—age, death—enter the mind. They are not even thoughts, but rather a growing surprise which, with time, turns into a certainty: that here is the truth. Then one takes stock of one's strength, and only then does one realize that it is insufficient, that we are not yet ready—which we knew, we knew it from the beginning. Yet during all that time we were preparing ourselves for something different, for something less important, for details. We called it action. We had it hammered in, repeated *ad infinitum*, that man realizes himself in action. In truth, in the country I come from, no one realizes himself in action, because action there takes place in spite of people or outside them. Individual acts are superfluous, even somewhat ill-advised, because what defines reality is another principle, based on self-sustaining self-imitation. One might, therefore, think that, in such a world, the ties between man and death would be more congenial and stronger, since life, being neither romantic nor engrossing, does not conceal death from him. And yet this is not the case. There, too, no one is prepared or better prepared. And what is worse, none are more interested.

If there had been one more question in the study—the

second whose absence seems to me unfortunate—if, I say, there had been a question about my relation to death, I would have liked the briefest possible wording: Are you prepared for death? And I would have replied, "No. Yet each day it interests me more."

So far, death and I have had only psychological relations with each other. My idea of death is the product of my imagination, of words and rituals. A certain distance still separates us, a little time and a hurdle of ignorance hard to get over. We get to know each other better at funerals, but, in fact, at those times it is more a question of closer ties with life. Someone has just died, we carry his coffin and his body, we play a little music and we stand among the trees, surrounded by familiar faces. So-and-so has left us, but that does not mean that we know death any better afterward. It is not us for whom the bell tolls, always for someone else. If one wished to keep count, how often during the week do we think about death? I know I devote more time to the business which awaits me next week. The day of my death is the boundary of my future, just as my birth is the boundary of my past. But I touch neither of these points in my experience; both are external to me. To be sure, my entire life should be an uninterrupted effort to build between these two points, from which I am cut off, a sort of bridge. As I leave the first to reach the second, I experience the irreversible, the fear of leaving myself. Each of my "next weeks," each of my "tomorrows" contains a particle of this fear, is a reflection of my fear of the end, and is the substitute for my experiencing death. My sole knowledge of it is indirect. I know neither origin nor destination, but only the scale of my possibilities. The future is an unknown my mind is able to grasp: I know I am falling into an abyss, but since I know it, it means that the abyss is not yet the total void.

Sometimes I can guess where the catch is; it is that eternity and nothingness have the same meaning for me and arouse the same fear. So much for us rationalists! We pay for the Age of Reason by the Age of Fear.

For my part I think that a certain change of perspective on life would be useful. I would describe it as choosing from the "point of view of death." It would consist in viewing one's life by standing at the end of it, and then living and acting in a way that would not be in too absurd and grotesque a contrast with that end. One would live "for the past," the end justifying the performance all the way back to its beginning, to its origin. In general, the perspective is just the opposite; one considers life from the moment of birth, the beginning is the point of departure, and the performance goes forward without end or limit. One lives "for the future." As I see it, this common perspective favors civilization, it encourages undertaking and risk, it promotes the game. Contrariwise, for culture, the perspective of death is the most fertile, in that it substitutes constructiveness for gambling, while the consciousness of fate that it implies broadens the horizons of life.

I am saying that civilization has no use for death, and yet we both know that our civilization holds the world record in the production of death. We also know that ideology, technology, and the exact sciences have all contributed to that production. It is extraordinary to think that for us the word *atom* is associated with annihilation and that the words *socialism* and *nation* suggest an enclosure under guard, containers filled with human bones, and a gate over which stand the words *Work* and *Freedom*. After such events, culture can no longer coexist with death. I speak of coexistence because, after all, the responsibility of culture is to acclimate the

114

individual to death, to disclose their family relationship. We know this much: that if death did not exist, life would have no meaning; it is through the knowledge of death that a value can be given to life. But death gives us access to the level of the gods, it alone permits culture to recognize that plane and understand it. It is to the death of one man that for almost two thousand years we have owed our idea of life, it is from having understood it that the culture of our world was born. All the same, when it is human endeavor that sets about producing death, culture can no longer bother with it. I am thinking of the millions of people who, during our lifetime, died in concentration camps and arctic deserts. The culture of future centuries will not dwell on their mass death, so engrossed will it be in another subject, larger and older, which is the capacity of one man to endure the death of another. To be able to endure the death of another is the first prerequisite of murder. To know that someone is dying and to continue to live, that is what opens the way to exterminating an entire nation. Culture does not feed on numbers. But are you sure that culture still survives in our time? Perhaps what looks to us like the culture of today is only the various ways of unburdening ourselves of the responsibility for all the deaths produced by civilization. "In the past there lived poets, the world was like a tree and they like children." Someone from our country wrote those words not very long ago. In the past, reality used to surround man with a circle of shadow as natural as light, and death was neighbor to life. In the past—before we invented the technology of death.

Chapter 8

I SHOULD LIKE to take up yesterday's topic again. Question twenty-one of the study is not unrelated to the question of death. It is phrased like this: *What is your greatest fear? What thought, imagining, consciousness, or fact most frequently puts you into a state of fear? And as to that state, would you describe it as arising from nature or metaphysics?*

Neither from nature nor from metaphysics. First, my fears are not connected with the thought of death. What I fear most is the problems of life, and those can arise even when you are in the best of health. If I had to give an unequivocal and short answer, I would describe my great fear as the *fear of provocation*. Let me explain by giving examples, some facts. I have already told you about an incident which occurred while I was working as a director in Wroclaw, when I encouraged an author to hide his play in his desk drawer. A week later, I received a visit which I will describe as discreetly official. The security forces were interested in our author and asked me to give them a copy of the play. When I explained that I did not have one in my possession, they suggested that I ask the author to return it with a view to a "second reading." Fifteen minutes later, I was in a taxi. The author listened as I repeated the conversation to him word for word and advised him either to bury his copy in the ground or to see that it disappeared from his house. I was not privileged with any more visits. As for the author, they left him alone. I spent a few more weeks serving the culture of the region before I was given to understand that it would be convenient for me, without stopping work as a director altogether, to give up my full-time job in the theater. I returned to Warsaw shortly thereafter.

Five years later, in Warsaw, this same author—who had meanwhile rewritten his play—informed me that only three people had had a copy of it at the earlier time, he, his wife, and I. Accordingly, he had wondered who could have put the security forces on the track of his work and its contents. He seemed to exclude the possibility that he or his wife had mentioned it somewhere or other. Anyhow, I understood that he suspected me, at the very least, of having been indiscreet. Would he not have suspected me of something worse, if, after I had returned my copy to him, the security forces had gone to him and not to me and had fished out his text from the drawer where I had advised him to hide it? Why didn't it happen that way? Probably because in every trade there is an artistic side, a subtle method of refining the style, and this refinement is all the more necessary when the nail is not to be driven all the way in. No doubt they only wanted to frighten the author, and as far as I was concerned their aim was twofold: to land me in a position where I would be forced to compromise myself and thus push me into dependence. Because they had come to me directly, the aim was only partly achieved, which perhaps was also part of the plan. But there is still a thought which torments me: if the management of the theater had suggested it, I would have asked the author in complete good faith for a copy of his work. I shudder to think of it. Hence what I call the fear of *provocation*. When, last year, in the boardinghouse where I was spending my vacation, there was a ring stolen from one of the rooms, my first thought was to lock my door before going down to dinner. You will say that that is an entirely normal reaction to the situation. I agree, but with this *amendment*: the idea of locking my room had nothing to do with any fear of being robbed. It was something else I was afraid of: that, during the meal, someone would put the stolen ring in *my* room. It would seem that we are less afraid of what must happen than of what can be done to us. In the first instance, there is only one possible outcome; in the second, the list of possibilities is infinite. I say "we," and I am thinking of the people of our two hemispheres. It will be more and more difficult to distinguish these people because it is the same pyramid which is being built, on different sides, with different methods. And on both sides, it is the masses who are building it. For this there is no need of slave drivers or guard towers. It is against themselves that the masses erect this pyramid. By whom—and indeed where— could our present-day world be compared to a tree? You remember the walk we took? We were talking about the inhumanity of today's cities and we came to the conclusion that beavers build their houses more intelligently than we do. You added a few words which I remember. I can't reproduce them exactly, but I give you the gist. You said: "For the first time we have discovered energy capable of destroying the planet and it is this same energy which for the first time allows us to leave it. We have forged new principles of social equality and we now see that they have engendered new tyrannies, better

119

organized than the old ones. Contemporary science has gone more deeply into the structure of matter, and the result is that it has reached the threshold of metaphysics." You spoke about these phenomena as being highly characteristic. Never before—and these are your words—"has man been so radically confronted with the laws of his own species." And you asked me for my opinion, whether I did not consider that we were at the end of a cycle. In such situations one tends to match ideas about Sumerian civilization or on the culture of the Mayas. But I, actually, I reacted differently. I told you that I do not make my daily bread out of such thoughts, the decline of our world rarely keeps me wakeful. If I remember correctly, you then began to talk about something else. I understand why. You probably found my reply a little harsh. But it wasn't so. It was I who felt surprised by your question. Where I live, we are not responsible for humanity. The history of the country has produced a peculiar state of mind which could be defined as wishing to free itself of all responsibility. In a country that was crossed off the map of the world for a century and a half, the relationship to the world cannot help having changed. Participation in the universal—humanity, progress, civilization—became less and less concrete as participation in the interests and work of humanity as a whole diminished. The world knew less and less about us, and we about the world. That is how a certain type of human being developed, living outside the universal and with whom, unquestionably, I have something in common. Believe me, no one in Poland has any illusions about contributing to the destiny of the world; everyone has the feeling—and it is an hereditary feeling—of being a foreigner to the age, of having missed the mainstream. And I tell you, it's an old, old story. From it have sprung complexes, longings, false ideas, and tragic evasions—and over and over again because we had no real links with the world. Three hundred years ago, Poland exerted no influence on the future of Europe, but the Polish people could still believe that they were saving Europe from Islam. Even thirty years ago, they could regard themselves as inspiring humanity in the fight against Hitlerism. But during the last thirty years, they have acquired a clearer perception of their condition as a plaything of history. That is a belief shared by bus driver and passenger alike. Both know that the world is changing; but if you ask them what is changing in Poland, they would reply: *nothing*. Because in Poland— they would explain—nothing *can* change. And the only right way of interpreting this is that in Poland, *they* are not able to change anything. They do not mean to imply that in thirty years the country has not known economic and social changes. The lesson goes deeper than that: all the changes that take place originate somewhere other than in the energies of the society and the initiative of individuals. It is self-evident, it is fundamental, and we live in the knowledge of it. If you were to question an intelligent journalist on the subject, he would answer you with figures—the amount of development, of growth, of progress, all in figures that are probably correct. The bus driver and his passenger learn these figures from the radio or television. Figures take the place of ideas. It appears from them that in industrial production, we are among the leading nations. And so, no doubt, in other things. But let's not on this account conclude that we have any importance for the world. The mass media function in only one direction, toward the public. Every day, they provide as fodder to millions of people news selected and digested in such a way as to make any critical judgment futile. The news is sold like merchandise, processed and packaged. You will say that this is a universal fact, that in today's world news is never "pure." I agree, but, just the same, there remains here and there the possibility of rejecting or accepting it after scrutiny. In the world I live in, that possibility is gone: television, radio, and the press have a monopoly on the choice and evaluation of all news. In reality the media form a censorship by sound track, a brilliant invention which drowns out reality by creating an acoustical barrier. If the women are fighting with each other in long lines outside the butcher shops in the morning, in the evening the television announcer talks about the tonnage produced in the shipyards.

At the same time, they make sure that society continues to believe it has not lost its ancient traits. The traditions of the Uhlans, the slogans of positivism, romanticism, nationalism, and revolution, the world of the Hussars—it is as if all this continued to be. The concepts and ideas which in centuries of struggle shaped the dreams and the experiences of that society are now released in one controlled flow—in the same way that the public is fed agricultural production statistics and news of unemployment in England. Thus a stream of information is designed to forestall public awareness and to create the illusion that it is the mere articulation of the public's voice. This is not just a propaganda trick, not just a way of subjecting millions to the concentrated suggestion of arguments and slogans. Its real purpose is to have millions of people live in the belief that they originate public opinion and that it is therefore real. It is a kind of manufactured collective voice heard on a closed circuit.

Here we are, at the heart of the problem. Do you know what we really lack? Do you know why the students from

Warsaw who clean the poultry in Paris cafeterias say that they suffer from claustrophobia in their own country? It is because the artificial quality of life makes one ill. Obviously, a variety of factors is needed for a society to occupy a real place in the sun and feel its own worth. Sixteenth-century Poland lived within its "rights," and France, from the Revolution to the fall of the Empire, in "history." As for the United States, they have lived the past hundred years in "civilization." I am using standard abbreviations of thought here, but I do not think that the matter can be stated any better. As for Polish reality, it is now situated in a supervised spot, where rights, history, and civilization do not, for the individual, fulfill their psychological role and do not engender higher forms of life. In a place where there are no heroes and no communion in the collective drama, existence is merely an anonymous day-after-day. The world around us is shaken by disturbances, it is headed in a certain direction, perhaps running toward its own destruction; but as for us, nothing depends on us, we can exert no influence on anything. Why, then, should I be thinking about causes outside of me? And if I did think about them, what use would my thoughts be? It would only confirm my powerlessness.

If from what I have just said you conclude that I live in a country run by a computer, you are wrong. I'm afraid I may have given you that impression. Actually, the country is run by a caste of managers who are beyond the control of society. Nobody expects an administration to have a noble soul. Let it be reasonable on the whole and we would be content. But instead of that it is conspicuous by its taste for petty prestige, by its wastefulness and its stupidities. Its members are appointed, and they are not recruited from among the most worthwhile elements of society. The word is "negative selection." To get ahead, one must be compliant; the sieve does not allow critical minds to pass through. I do not know if you realize the unbelievable absurdities of which the bureaucracies of the East are capable. You have to read the Russians, they know what it is like. Herzen, in his memoirs, described the "potato revolt" in the Kazan region. In the beginning, the peasants of every country planted potatoes without enthusiasm; they held this invention in very low esteem. In the eighteenth century, the French government, wishing to promote this new crop, ordered all its agents to have potatoes planted, while officially and absolutely forbidding them to give any to the peasants. And those same agents received unofficial instructions to close their eyes to any thefts. Since potatoes had become a forbidden vegetable, all the parishes of France were soon covered with them. A few decades later the Russian government resorted to force to solve the same problem. The Russian peasants also hated potatoes but the government ordered them to be planted. Then they decided to have great holes dug where the potatoes could be buried during the winter months. Despairing, the peasants dug the holes and brought the potatoes. The vegetables froze. In the spring, when the government ordered the frozen tubers planted, the peasants refused. This was seen as a revolt. The army was sent out. They sprayed the villages with bullets, and cossack battalions took prisoner the peasants found hiding in the woods. The potato revolt ended in deportations to Siberia. To understand the full absurdity of this scheme, you have to know Russian history. And to understand the most recent history of Poland, you have to remember that the model of our government is imported from Russia, and that the system, to top it all off, is the work of those same potato-fed sons of peasants. No doubt Herzen would have been plunged into meditation by this historical irony; he did not foresee it.

For the last twenty years Herzen's memoirs have not been reprinted here because of the sinister picture of Russia which they give. He was one of those spotless characters of the nineteenth century who could reply, like Proudhon to Thiers when the latter had insulted him in the Assemblée Nationale: "I will not challenge you to a duel, not I. But I will, from this podium, tell you the story of my entire life, deed by deed. Anyone may call me to order if I forget or distort anything, and then you can get up and do the same."

What is the most surprising is that from Herzen's time, in Russia and elsewhere, men here and there have been frightened at the thought of an Eastern Communism which, as was obvious enough, had become an historical reality. Dostoyevsky foresaw the Russian revolution as a combination of jails, provocations, and nihilist sects. At the same period, in his letters from the heart of Normandy, Flaubert was writing that Communism would imprison man in barracks painted dirty yellow, would stupefy him, would reduce him to the two acts of chewing his food and defecating, would deny him all higher thoughts. He went on to say that in his opinion, Russia would swallow Western Europe as she had swallowed Poland. Herzen himself feared a regime under which "men would be like prisoners condemned to equality." Dire prophecies, therefore, surrounded the monster's cradle from the moment of its birth. And all this was written with reference to Poland, in Herzen as in Flaubert. The Poles themselves knew Russia like Occidentals and knew what to think about her. It is also true that the Poles of today would have a great deal to say to the French as well as to the Russians.

I suppose you take me for a representative of the Polish intelligentsia, that enlightened and patriotic social class that has a tradition of taking upon itself the spiritual guidance of the nation, of making men out of the Polish people and of determining the place of Poland in the world. Indeed, your questionnaire has a paragraph along these lines, and the question you ask is an important one: *Does your social existence condition your thinking, and if so, to what extent? Do you see yourself as a product of your membership in a class?—or to an ethnic, professional, or religious group?*

One might think that a Marxist had written this section of the questionnaire. It is striking to observe how profoundly the Marxist categories have penetrated your mind, the humanist mind. There is a paradox here: the perpetuation of Marx's social ideas is now the work of the developed capitalist countries, while we, instead of building our socialist superstructures as Marxists, are the ones who yearn for metaphysics. I often think that it would be in one of your universities that one would find the young Marx teaching today.

The Polish intelligentsia . . . I sometimes wonder if the philosophy of our nation, its energy and its reserves of psychological strength—if all this does not get dissipated in wit and whispered jokes, anonymous, always mocking, ironic, or absurd, often couched in a sentence or two; if for us these things have not begun to take the place of thought, courage, and dignity. For instance: "Rabbi, can one build socialism in only one country?" "Yes, my son, one can build socialism in only one country, but one must live in another." It's a very old joke, almost a classic of its kind. But who do you think made it up? And who makes up the hundreds of others? Without a doubt, some very intelligent people. There's no trace of popular humor there; they're inventions of the intelligentsia. As you can see, we are still busy with the guidance of souls!

YESTERDAY I TALKED to you about the intelligentsia. What does it mean in Poland today to belong to the intelligentsia? Who belongs to it? That's what nobody knows. Sometimes, in an attempt to be precise, one speaks of the humanist intelligentsia, or "the intellectuals." But the lack of criteria makes the situation anything but plain. No one knows who belongs to the intelligentsia because no one knows what it is. One simply knows that it is no longer what it was fifty or a hundred years ago. Of course, certain remarks can be made, especially in the form of pious wishes. One can, for example, assert that the intelligentsia is a social class that creates the consciousness society has of itself; or again, that it constitutes a certain type of human being who puts culture ahead of reality. It sounds right, but it is inadequate, it is too subjective. Who takes on this role of social consciousness, how, when, and where? Is it journalists in the daily papers or Ph.D.'s in the weeklies? Who puts culture ahead of reality, and for whom is it the other way around? How must we organize and conduct research—by means of surveys and confessions? Gone are the old objective criteria by which it appeared that the schoolteacher, the physician, and the judge helped to make up the intelligentsia for reasons beyond their own intellectual ambitions, because the mere fact of being a doctor, a teacher, or a judge defined one's place in society. Do you remember the schoolmasters of the time before the war? Do you recall what the funeral of the old doctor meant in a small town? To me in the thirties, the position of judge was still endowed with the prestige inherent in justice. These characters may have looked overfed, they were often riddled with faults, sometimes even ridiculous or eccentric. But for us their professions were still associated with the accepted idea of *homo sapiens*; they symbolized broad-mindedness, justice, aid to the needy. They themselves could be far from perfect, and sometimes we would curse our teachers, doctors, and judges. But within us still beats a common human understanding. What's happened exactly? Can our doctors, our teachers, and our judges be worse than they were? Should we give more authority to the intelligentsia or educate people differently?

I have already said that the war could have given the Polish people the opportunity to find themselves. The occupation, to be sure, served to reveal the heroism of the people but also their smallness. The conflict illuminated the heart of man. Society came out of the war bloodstained and traumatized: we were not dead, but we had witnessed the death of others. It was not the rule to be forced to choose between one's own death and that of another; that didn't happen to everybody every day. But everybody knew a neighbor who had been murdered. Every little village had had its share of massacres, massacres followed by silence. It was the work of foreigners, but it took place here. It left a deeply troubled memory and conscience. A Christian conscience, and disturbed at the thought that the laws of morality and mercy could be flouted in this way. For of course everyone knew during those years that he slept next door to a torture chamber and that heaven was silent. Right after the war, these experiences began to be recalled in literature; it was the voice of the Polish intelligentsia first making itself heard after the night. Then silence again, by tacit agreement; the subject was in disrepute; the war meant the army, the underground, and the fight with the enemy. Only small printings were made of books about "the Age of Crematoriums." I do not bring this up casually: I am giving an indication of how the intelligentsia was reduced to silence. Any subject relating to ethics in its aspect of universal truth is suppressed by the system because it likes only what is functional—the catechism instead of the Gospel. The machine does not like the complications raised by intellectuals; it does not tolerate questions that are not on the agenda, spontaneous questions from the floor. Questions must be addressed to the presidium in writing, and preferably before the meeting. In this way the intelligentsia is deprived of its habitual way of life; open discussion, public exchange of ideas, the fight for social conscience and its own dignity. It cannot express its genuine thoughts on the problems of the people, the country, and the world. The Poles and the Russians, the Poles and the Jews, the Poles and the West, recent Polish history, the problem of the nation's destiny—as many subjects that once used to make up the tradition of thought of our intelligentsia and that are prohibited today. Nothing is left but journalistic talk on the role of the contemporary intellectual in the construction of the socialist world, but these parodies of true discussion deal with everything except what is of interest to everybody. There is no other choice than solitude or a second life in the realm of appearances. You want to know how such an existence is possible? Well, then, one lives oneself out as a superfluous being in the Organized Lie.

One might ask how an intelligent man in Poland *should* live today. He must work at his profession. There surely are circles in society where responsibilities are a function of talent and experience, and in each profession there must be a meeting place between strictly professional issues and the interests of society as a whole. Every intelligent man in Poland who wishes to practice his profession in accordance with these interests encounters in his path a politico-administrative structure. If, for example, he is a professor of history, he must stick to the official interpretation of events and ignore the most recent facts in the history of the country. In the high school and at the university he had already run up against the operation of this same structure—that is the circle in which he moves. Should he want to extricate himself, he could do it only at the cost of an enormous effort. He finds the ubiquitous rigidity often comic in that it contradicts the whole environment. He has to be afraid of principles, because everything he knows, observes, or imagines propels him toward compromise and resignation. He knows whom he is measuring himself against, he knows that he is a loser, having seen how others have lost. He is therefore besieged from outside and conquered from within at the same time; he thinks against himself, marked with the seal of defeat, which has kept up with him at every step. Should he refuse to be resigned, not only will he ruin his career, but he will fall into a void. And nobody can tell ahead of time the strength of his resistance to a void—can say if he is able to withstand it. That is an annihilating thought; it sends one back into the unknown, the life which it promises is as if disembodied. The intelligent man who shrinks from this unknown becomes a *practical* man. He can then choose among a few varieties of *practical* life. He can also stuff his ears and shut himself up in his specialty. He can even show his inner revolt by some slight gesture. If he belongs to the chosen caste, he can haul himself up into the position of a favorite while maintaining his extraterritoriality. Everything depends on his cleverness and the area in which he works. In any event, from then on he will be taken in, and after a time will be awarded a prize or a medal—you must imagine here the decorations put on horses in the stable. He will be "functional." If, however, he rejects compromise, he will find himself face to face with a powerful adversary. I don't mean that, forgive me, I am putting it badly: his antagonist has more than one face; it is the mass of society.

Chapter 9

To FOLLOW UP my statement on the intelligentsia, I should like to connect up with question twenty-four of the survey: *Define the social differences in your country. Is there a privileged class? What are its characteristics and the reasons for its privileges?*

I am quite incapable of producing a sociological analysis of the class structure which stratifies the population of my country. I find it a good deal easier to answer the second part of the question. A privileged class there most certainly is; it is found, first of all, in the politico-administrative machine and its various offshoots. That is the dividing line. The nature of their privileges? All the advantages that derive from unlimited power, for instance: impunity, the right to use violence, the power to interfere in all spheres of life, personal immunity guaranteed by the hierarchy.

Between this group and the rest of the population, it happens that some links develop through a sort of osmosis. Dependency does not always exclude interpenetration. I have often noticed it in my own area, the theater. But at the same time there remains a psychological gap, felt by both sides. The people, which form the majority, realize that their vital interests do not constitute for the ruling apparatus any absolute guide to action; they know they are subordinate to the interests of power. The machine knows it, too: society provides the raw materials of its activities and it could not do without it, but the true life of the machine is the inner workings of the hierarchy. And the activity of the organization is only a means to which the game of the struggle for power gives meaning. The two sides are aware of this; each regards the presence of the other as a necessity which it must reckon with; each adopts toward the other tactics based on deceit and evasion. Society has learned to keep quiet; the machine knows that it must talk about something else. The truth is like a secret known to everyone; falsification is a shared reality. When there is a shortage of goods in the shops, the citizen understands that he cannot ask for explanations from authority; it isn't worth it. Authority works on the same assumption—that it is not worth it: not worth giving the citizen reasons for the inadequate supply, because they are too complicated or too incriminating; more often than not they reveal the political dependence of the state. The upshot is that authority talks about folk dancing and the rate of industrial growth. The machine suffers from both a superiority and an inferiority complex. It is the ruling caste who have at hand the verified information about the state's dependency. They know best to what necessities they must yield. These are state secrets, and by comparison complaints from consumers seem childish. In their eyes criticism is always irresponsible and never proves anything except the ignorance of the person who utters it. Real reasons cannot be disclosed; they form the substance of an hermetically sealed knowledge, they constitute a code in the service of authority. Officials live in the shadow of their superiors; they carry on their gamble in an increasingly rarefied atmosphere, it is their life, their passion, while down below society continues to live and to bustle about.

Still, criticism coming from below is an offense in that it touches them on the sore spot of their inferiority complex. The administration is aware of not being the product of an election and knows that its existence is only guaranteed from outside. Not only does the administration know this, but it also knows that society is aware of it. This shared awareness puts salt on the wound. The machine is on the defensive, it never stops denying its mistakes, its abuses, and its absurdities, but it must also produce proofs of its authenticity, of its ties with the country—hence, the folk dancing. This contrived effort at authenticity only aggravates the lie. If the people were kept informed of the reasons for the shortages in the stores, it would be a genuine moment in the relationship between the government and its citizens. Folk dances are beautiful, but when they are made to take the place of information they give rise to fury. This is how the shortage of information led to an anecdote on shortages of goods: "We send clay pigeons to Hungary; in exchange we receive eggs. We send the eggs to Czechoslovakia and in exchange we receive chickens. We sell the chickens in Bulgaria in exchange for chicken-liver pâté. We export this pâté to the Soviet Union, which sends us back clay pigeons."

It is a sanctified principle to suppress the truth. There was a time when it surprised me. I did not think that anyone could be so simple-minded or so shameless as to think that society accepted at face value all this counterfeit news whose only function is to conceal the real facts. What's the use, since everybody ends up finding out about them anyway? Why not make public the circumstances of the massacre of the Polish officers at Katyn when there is not a single Pole, starting with the party members holding the highest posts, who does not know that they were shot by officers of the NKVD? By the same token, I could not understand why nothing was said of the reasons for the short supplies, since those who wait in line would be less irritated if it were explained to them why they get bad quality meat. Yet no information is given about the reasons or even about the fact that such problems exist; and you can be sure that if this is the case it is not by accident or lack of awareness. If there is anything that is deliberate and knowingly and consistently protected it is the principle of not dealing with the truth. One might think that this was a silly mistake for the machine to make. When, for example, a cheap item disappears from the stores, one can be sure that it will reappear a week later relabeled and at a higher price. In the streets they say that such products have been "rebaptized," and they complain; but the newspapers publish joyful news about the novelty and beauty of the packaging. . . .

It seems impossible to follow a more absurd policy. Or so I thought for a long time, but there is no doubt that I was wrong. There is nothing stupid about it at all. From the point of view of those who govern it is not stupid. What has no name is always less dangerous than what has one, because it is words that convert facts into social forces. The Eastern bureaucracies have always known this. They know that to call something by its real name amounts to giving it life. Experienced criminals also know this: they never admit to being guilty unless they are caught red-handed—otherwise they stubbornly deny everything. The power machine is caught red-handed every day, and every day shamelessly denies it. The analogy is instructive: criminals and politicians do not belong to the same class, yet it remains true to say that their methods are related.

Only to us does telling the truth look like the best method. We fail to appreciate the magic that consists in changing the facts, in calling black "white" in front of millions of people who know how to tell one color from another. We joke about this vulgar magic, but we ourselves are its victims and it makes us impotent. The reason is our silence. For in one way or another we are silent, we do not open our mouths to say publicly what we know and think, and what *they themselves* know. And does not this mean that *they* have achieved their goal? We can boast about perceptiveness and congratulate ourselves on not being asses—no, you see, we didn't get taken in. But neither can we bray or kick: we have fallen under the curse, we have the heads of asses. As to our daily behavior, it is—oh, so reasonable.

It is reasonable, because rights, ethical feeling, collective and individual, as well as the principles of life and thought based on the notion that the human community has value—all have given way to the *practicality* of the governors and the governed. The new power does not respect the laws that limit it, and society responds in the same way. There are no brakes in that area and it would be a serious mistake to think that the Poles of today are a religious nation. Practicality is the soul of both public and private affairs: to live means to act efficiently, that is, to attain one's goals. These are society's criteria and they are almost universal. Why? Because—tell me where any others are to be found? It is a vicious circle; the actions of the state toward society and of society toward the state take place outside the law—it is all the same thing whether one goes from top to bottom or from bottom to top. And if in spite of these conditions, in spite of everything, material progress for the masses is achieved, it is again at the price of new perversions in the modes of thought. Such is approximately the environment available to an intelligent Pole today. Obviously I give here nothing more than a rough, incomplete outline.

I am suddenly reminded of a funeral. It was a funeral without priests, with a distinguished attendance and medals on a cushion. I do not remember the season; it was probably toward the end of autumn or early winter. Anyhow, it was neither very warm nor very cold. Truth to tell, this funeral was almost indistinguishable from other ordinary funerals held at state expense. Perhaps there were a few more people. I had gone with my daughter and we met Icz along the cemetery walk. Mewa was still in high school; she had asked me to take her because the deceased had read his verses at her school one evening, and she remembered them. I also recall that Icz, who was beside us, had whispered something that irritated me. I think it was about the end of the Era of Pathos, or something like that. He would not let me go and kept repeating endlessly that there was in it something extremely interesting. I did not understand what he meant, and try as I might to pay attention to the ceremony, I kept seeing the same bare heads, the same faces. His rhetoric had always got on my nerves. Later he accosted me in the streetcar and explained to me what he really had in mind. It was that the death of the deceased—whom he called by his nickname—had brought to a close the era when revolution harked back to a romantic past—he termed it "the appeal to blood and to ideas," and from that moment the intelligentsia had ceased to be necessary. For what had drawn the intelligentsia into the revolution, the ethical and social slogans, the abolition of exploitation and injustice—all that could almost be considered accomplished, so that in the years ahead we would enter a new phase which Icz described as that of peasant utilitarianism. In the future, the intelligentsia would become an expropriated class, it would have to pay for its revolutionary programs, for its ideas and its theories—for its ideology. He did mention Marx, Freud, and Einstein; he referred to them as the founders of the twentieth century, "three Jews who deprived humanity of God." Those are the very words he used, if I remember correctly, and I think I do remember correctly.

The point isn't what Icz said, anyway. What is important is that I did not try to advance a single one of my ideas against what he was saying. I sensed Mewa's penetrating gaze on me, as if she was amused or surprised that I did not start a debate; but really I had not the slightest urge to do so. Later, in the restaurant, I ate a piece of meat and watched the people sitting around. I should at least have smiled at my daughter, since I did not want to talk, and I could also have got rid of Icz with a pun or a shrug of the shoulders. Instead of that, nothing. I did not utter a word! And once again, the important thing is not what Icz said, but my reaction, which provides much food for thought. Of course, I couldn't account for it at once or the next day; but with the passage of time I can offer a conjecture: namely, unconsciously I thought that Icz was right and at the same time I regarded his words as off the point. Icz was expounding a theory of reality, and probably he was not mistaken in his views. If that had been all, it should have been easy to agree. And yet I was on the defensive. In keeping silent I was saying no, once and for all, to what was challenging me from outside in the guise of a truth that claimed to include me and to define me without caring what its psychological meaning might be for me. I did not, therefore, care to find out if it confirmed my inner truth or if it reduced it to nothingness.

In short: I had had enough. I already felt tired of this tension between myself and the age, between myself and the facts and their various interpretations. I was even becoming indifferent to everything that was solidly based on history, all that was capable of convincing me intellectually, and which had its justification if not in me, at least in its relationship to me. That was my moment of refusal, or breaking off. Of course, it had been coming over me for a long time, but on that day—and it is only now that I fully realize it—it was final. As you know, such moments can be very important without its showing immediately on the outside.

As I just told you: refusal or breaking off. I want to make sure that you don't misunderstand me. It was not a break on my side. Only a dreamer could see the victory of the Allies as the victory of ideas over brute force. The actual victory was one of logistics, the supply of fuel, the production of machines. But everyone felt the need of a reality defined in different terms, and everyone was ready to adapt to new principles of life in common. This need arose from the fact that everyone's consciousness had been disoriented, that after the war no one could consider himself innocent, that everyone had lost all sense of his individual importance. Everyone expected that the law coming from outside would take the form of a general code. I am speaking of myself, as well; I, too, was ready to adapt to it, and I accepted the possibility of personal failure as the price of a new order. But I quickly saw my mistake. There was no common ground between my attitude toward reality and reality itself; nothing then being done needed my advice, my desire, my beliefs. I eventually came to the conclusion that it would be just that kind of system which would become the new principle of social life and would take the place of the one we were expecting. Thus, it was not I who broke with reality. It would be closer to the truth to say that reality broke with me.

It was imperative to draw the consequences of all this, and I drew them. I was sure when I bought the daily papers that none of their articles could jibe with my way of thinking, and that none of them were conceived in order to urge me to take any individual action. It was as if the writers were addressing themselves above my head to powers whose point of view they knew in advance. All that was left for me to do was to accept this collective machinery which took the place of thought and action. Every article confirmed my suspicion that the paper was not written for me or for anyone else, and that it performed no useful function except among the hierarchical powers. I surprised myself one day by finding that I was only reading the obituaries. That someone had just died comforted me by the objectivity of the report; it was the only place where life came through. The obituary columns were free of editorial comments, consisting only of brief biographical particulars from which it would emerge, for example, that a certain individual had been an officer in 1939 or had been a victim, along with his wife, of an automobile accident. This information did not emanate from the newspaper staff, but from private individuals—parents, children, or friends. The objectivity of this conventional form proved indescribably fascinating to me. It brought with it something original, an originality which took me some time to understand. The something was uniqueness. The obituaries avoided the anonymous collective style which was the rule in the other articles, about work in the coal mines, the population of the capital, and the plans of architects. Those other articles would maintain the illusion that the only *person*

141

in society was the state. One day I learned the new word *nomenclature*, as used in our administration: it designates those officials who are permitted to shed their anonymity and to be quoted in the news. Still, it is always in a personal way, in a limited edition of one copy, that one dies. An obituary can be a story: it has a hero, and that is how a first name and a last name, when framed in a black border, manage to escape censorship.

You think that my talk is full of exaggerations. Believe me, I, too, tried to reason that way with myself. But it is not in the guise of an embittered individualist that I am most comfortable. I said to myself: they are building houses for the workers, they are introducing free education and social security, the children of the peasants are learning to read, poverty is disappearing, nobody starves anymore. But all my efforts toward objectivity ended in a desire to know why the reforms undertaken in the interests of the workers necessarily excluded their right to a critical judgment, why the reforms were to be undertaken for them, why they could not be undertaken by them . . .

To tell the truth, that's the question with which every discussion should begin, whether it is about productivity, about education, or about the development of culture. But in Poland today no one can bring up such a question in public. It is an intellectual's question which brings one back to the theology of progress, and every man whose thought makes use of social categories must ask it of himself; it is the most revolutionary question that can be asked within a statist system. "It makes no sense," someone once said, "to draw a line through everything for the sake of the idea of equality." As for me, I wonder if equality, liberty, and justice can differ to that extent.

While I fully realize the differences that exist, I think

that this set of problems is not altogether dissimilar from those of the mass societies in your part of the world. Don't you agree that today's crises and changes in values, in the Communist as well as in the capitalist world, come from an inherent flaw in their philosophical bases? If we were to ponder the nature of these two great visions of social management, perhaps we would come to see them both as utopian; that is, both the system which regulates distribution according to work and needs, and the system which relies on the game of conflicting individual interests. I sometimes think that neither Smith nor Marx, with their confidence in progress and in man's creative potential, foresaw the self-destructive elements implied in them. Again, the French in 1789, when they proclaimed in a single breath their slogan, "Liberty, Equality, Fraternity," did not know that they were converting humanism into an obsession equivalent to perpetual motion in physics. From the viewpoint of the devil, Hitlerism was even simpler: in counting upon stupidity, cruelty, and fear, it was postulating from the outset the existence of destructive forces. And it liberated them first, in order later to govern with them.

Perhaps both of us, you and I, are the sons of utopia— very different from one another, certainly, but our anxiety is the same. Yet I do not feel that I am competent to analyze the reasons for this "analogy between differences." Nor do I nurse any such ambition; it is primarily my own position that I am analyzing.

Viewed from outside, my position had been clear for many years. I had a post in a university and in addition, theaters, particularly in the provinces, would often approach me to direct plays. But inside, let us say subjectively, I did not feel my position as stable as it looked. I constantly felt that I had not accomplished the most elementary of my duties toward reality: reality was doing without my spiritual participation, though I was living in it, existing in it. One can live that way. I was exaggerating when I described such a state as desperate. One stands it day after day, like having flat feet or chronic migraine; there is in it a combination of illness and boredom, a lack of satisfaction. One lives apart from the action, one suffers the wretchedness of imaginings that lead nowhere, one's surroundings become less and less distinct, their particularity is blurred. You end up by becoming indifferent to your own fate as one does with a dull novel one has read before. Such a life has a certain smoothness; there are fewer struggles and conflicts. One becomes soft. After a while I stopped buying the newspapers. I began to read memoirs—no matter whose, provided they talked about the past: lives already lived appealed to me; they were as if well-arranged by time, and especially, *lived otherwise*. I read fiction less frequently. It is discouraging at the best of times to compare your own experiences with those described in novels. There is nothing comforting about it.

And all around me new-style people were bustling about, eager to get ahead and prepared to push everyone else aside, unscrupulous and as calm and energetic as insects. I was witnessing the birth of a new type of Pole, briefcase in hand, stopping at nothing to obtain a thirteenth month's pay or a trip abroad. Souls were not expensive and were selling cheap. I also saw a new type of "good" Pole developing, always raising and lowering his hand at the same time as the presidium—a Pole who would never take a stand on any public issue. At most he would grumble the way my father did when I said to him, during a meal, that military honor was the invention of officers. I was already convinced that the majority of the people in my country lived with an amputated idea of liberty, and I was beginning to understand something: things go badly when rights are violated, but things are even worse when people forget the very nature of their rights. Theories, plain and *practical*, philosophies of bad faith, proliferated. One of these maintained that the best course was to *be quiet and persevere*, rather than to escape and give way to others, for the others would be worse. There was a more brutal attitude which tackled the problem head on: everything consists of crap, including ourselves, and only the hopeless idiots refer to moral principles; these in fact are the most dangerous types, they and their principles are the ones that must be trampled and buried in the crap, even if it means sitting on top of them. Don't imagine that these were philosophies professed by the workers alone; after a couple of drinks, humanists rallied to them in great numbers. I saw them on television. The set was to have been a surprise for Mewa after she passed her finals, but to tell the truth, it was for myself that I bought it. In order to see *them*, for exactly *that reason*. I took a wicked pleasure in their hypocrisy and the fear they betrayed. There is something fascinating in witnessing the loss of dignity, and after watching them, I came to think better of myself. Ah! To compare oneself *with them*—to me that was all they were good for! But this meant that life was losing its value. I wondered whether my own dignity continued to be anything more than a mirage, and whether I could afford the comfort of integrity at the price that was asked: holding my tongue.

And yet I say it again—life went on. Real despair, I remember, occurred during the war. In December 1944 when the crowd would sing in the churchyards, "Listen, Jesus, the people beseech you; Jesus, save us with a miracle!"—you don't know those songs?—well, then, that was despair, the people were really invoking the help of God. You could see freshly dug graves in those yards. But people today own apartments and television sets; they build private houses; restaurants, cinemas, theaters are packed; we go to the beach and to the mountains; in the street it is impossible to tell the difference between a manual worker and a college graduate, everybody dresses the same way and has the same rights. The miracle has occurred. Around 1970 the economists of the West spoke of "Poland's economic miracle." There has been, unquestionably, a general increase in wages and a rise in our standard of living.

My father, I may say, limited his idea of liberty to the nation itself—was *it* free? Now everybody says that freedom for the Poles comes down to supplying the butcher shops. That's the basis for deciding whether the nation is free. "We are an independent, free nation; we are good Polish citizens, we have beaten the Turks and the Germans—and the Muscovites as well (something which everyone secretly remembers). We have learned how to work and how to heed the power of the people." And the good Polish citizens, the docile Polish, both those who vote in unison with the presidium and those who grumble about political liberty, all reply to the machine, "Right you are, we are Poles, we fought at Grunwald, and now we want some ham." By waiting in line, by crowding into the shops, by forcing the power machine to satisfy their needs, by joining together to win the battle of goods and victuals, they raise the flag that symbolizes their right to better and higher consumption. That's what has become the fulfillment of a Polish citizen's duties. I am not joking, believe me. This is exactly the shape which the fight for national life has currently taken. It is a kind of technological substitute. The long line in front of the butcher shop means a stubborn will to defend our rights. Be that as it may, to say that for the Polish people of today, freedom is nothing more than a synonym for ham is— superficial . . .

Now you are going to ask me: When all is said and done, what's the point of all this?

Rights.

Ten years ago, I was approached by several foreign theaters, in Norway and Switzerland. The terms they offered were not at all bad. Since then, I have directed plays in quite a few cities in Western Europe where they take an interest in new dramatic and literary trends. Six years ago I was returning from Oslo to Warsaw after two months of exhausting work. I had succeeded in staging, without cuts, the entire *Romeo and Juliet*. It was the beginning of spring and it was cool. Nobody was at the airport to meet me, and the customs inspector had cut in half the bar of soap I had brought back among my toilet articles. The city I rode through was full of police and military patrols. At the same time I noticed that the traffic in the street was the same as usual. Shops, offices, and public transportation were all open and working, the streetcars were full of indifferent faces. It was at home that I found out what was going on: the banning of *Forefather's Eve* by Mickiewicz at the National Theater, the student strikes, the clamping down and arrests that followed. That night on television, I saw women dressed in white, workers in a sugar refinery, who were shouting at the camera and brandishing banners with slogans denouncing the anti-Polish plot and the Jewish conspirators. Was it all real? Had people gone mad during my absence? Those women had faces of fury; behind them others were lined up under placards.

In the morning I went down to buy the papers and,

after a moment's perusal, I had the impression that we had dug up the hatchet. One of my students, a boy crammed with talent, telephoned me; he had been expelled from the university for having taken part in the demonstration in the theater. He had been beaten with a club in the courtyard of the university. I asked him to come over that evening. He did not come, he had been arrested during the day. At the faculty meeting I asked that a petition be presented in his behalf. Then we went on to discuss the budget. As I was scribbling notes, I suddenly remembered what the story of *Forefather's Eve* was about: arresting students for conspiring. Now, one hundred and fifty years later, they were arresting students for conspiracy because they demonstrated against the banning of *Forefather's Eve*. It seemed to me then that history had a divine sense of irony. I kept silent during the rest of the meeting, but I wrote a letter. It was all I could do: a page and a half, typed, couched in the calm style of a petition. I sent the letter by mail to the Minister of Higher Education. A month later, they put a stop to my courses. As for my student, he was released after fourteen months' detention. He telephoned me again. We met in the botanical garden on a hot early afternoon; we both had plenty of time at our disposal. I chose a bench in the high part of the garden, the most unoccupied—it was there that I used to meet Rabczyn during the war to give him the latest intelligence from the command.

Which of us two found the meeting more difficult? I don't know. Perhaps he did not expect me to offer any answer. We were both at the same dead end, sitting on a bench like two colleagues. Of course he had ahead of him almost as many years of thought as I had behind me, but on that day our respective wisdoms could not be measured. The day seemed to trail along the ground, smothered by a filthy hand. Have you experienced those moments of helplessness when you can neither open your mouth nor lift a finger? The thought crossed my mind that both of us had had our hands cut off, and that neither of us would have been able to give the other a glass of water. We had both been deprived of our rights.

I guessed that after a while they would take him back at the university, that he would complete his studies and receive his degree in play directing; that then he would leave for the provinces, where a theater would employ him. In my thought, the world for him had been reduced to a pile of dirty tricks, and I had no desire to explain to him the ways of the world. The most I could say to him was: If you think now that the world is unworthy of you, in a year you will think it is unworthy of your regrets. And in two years they will buy you. They will give you a briefcase, a desk, and a car. I will see you on television expounding your latest ideas about the world and about art. Yet I knew that was not what was lying in wait for him. He had probably decided *to wait*. To wait for what? A change, a passport, a miracle? Or maybe for a new prophet? I could also have told him to look to his own salvation. But all I said was that I was asking myself these same questions and that, right then, I had no desire to persuade anyone. I spoke to him more or less in these words: "You got a blow on the head which has spurred you to think. Let us suppose they give you a job and you go to Zielona Góra, or they give you a passport and you leave for the West. You will take your head with you and I shall stay here with mine. But our two heads should remember one thing: even though they took away our rights, that does not mean that we are free to forget them. It is we, we alone who can alienate our rights, by ceasing to be aware of them, by forgetting them."

I had nothing more to say to him. Take it as an answer to question twenty-three: *If you had a chance to speak to delegates of the young from all over the world, what would be the tenor of your remarks? What would be the main thing you would talk to them about? How would you advise them and what would you tell them to guard against?*

Chapter 10

THIS MORNING a stranger whose name I did not catch telephoned me. It ended in -owski or -ewski. He spoke Polish and suggested that we meet. He said that he had heard on television of my arrival at the conference. During the sessions, the networks held short interviews with some of the members, myself included. When I asked him what he wanted to talk with me about, he said: "Ancient history—the war." And he added: "I was a member of 'Rondo.' " He said he had tried to get in touch with me several times but had not been able to reach me at the hotel. Tomorrow morning he will wait for me at the Iorgenshouve bar. I hope that I am not in for a kidnapping.

I spoke to you yesterday about what took place in Poland in March 1968 and afterward. The facts were fully reported and discussed in the West. You must have heard about them. It was at that time, you remember, that Czechoslovakia was experiencing its miracle, the Prague Spring—a miracle brutally cut short in August of the same year by the invasion of three armies, Russian, Polish, and East German. After the student arrests in Warsaw came the trial of the Prague intellectuals. In December 1970 the workers went on strike along the shores of the Baltic. Fights with the police and the army left many dead and wounded. The year 1971 saw the beginning of a new policy: the peasants were no longer forced to deliver, the price of staple goods was frozen, important commercial treaties were concluded with the West, and the construction of housing was accelerated. Wages were increased, the Polski Fiat went into production, and savings accounts rose every month. The number of tourists in Poland increased, as did the number of Polish travelers abroad. As I said, that was Poland's economic miracle, or, to put it more modestly, the reforms our people awaited.

But, you will recall, when I spoke about the emancipation of the peasants I mentioned the difficulties that had long stood in the way of this inevitable reform. It is not easy to compare the Russian reforms of 1850 with those made in Poland in 1970. Still, the "price" we paid for ours can roughly be assessed: arrests, convictions, heavy dismissals, the wave of emigration, the massacres of striking workers in the Baltic towns. The total cost is yet to be computed. The reinstatement of nationalist slogans and anti-Semitism in the press should be added to the list. In a country where the Germans exterminated three million Jews during the war, those who escaped the gas chambers learned from the newspapers that they were now foreigners in the land. Those were the words used in government circles; they did not have great social repercussions but they enabled certain people in the administration to snatch at swift advancement. Of the ideology there remained only the hackneyed language of the machine, in which expressions like "service to the nation" and "loyalty to the working class" both mean an attitude of complete submission to those in power. The model of the perfectly submissive man is becoming more and more common. His sins are forgiven because of his virtue, which lies in not thinking. This type of man has a long history which is described in the textbooks. You agree that the history of every nation has its periods of light and periods of shade. We have paid and continue to pay for a Poland silly and benighted; the Americans in 1963, when President Kennedy was assassinated, paid for a country silly and benighted, and are still paying for it. The ghosts in a seance come and go; the ghosts of history are more persistent.

The changes that took place in Poland after 1945 have been spoken of as the "gentle revolution." Gentle it certainly wasn't for everybody. But it did have the dimensions of a revolution. It came from outside, from Russia, and it remodeled the social structure of the country. Had it been allowed to draw upon the vital forces of the country, I think that a socialist Polish regime founded on rights could have been created. I repeat: had it been allowed. Optimists kept this hope alive for a long while, and in spite of everything the month of October 1956 reinforced that hope. Yet ten years after October I saw these same men psychologically broken. Only the cynics still spoke of ideology. In the land, illegality already infected everything. That condition lasted several years. When it became impossible to delay making changes, a few puppets were taken out of the cupboard and the lights were dimmed. The farce was performed in the dark. That was in 1968, after the students' month of March. When the Baltic towns erupted thirty months later and there began to be talk of "Renovation," hope returned to many of those I am talking about. That was after the workers' December, during the first few months of 1971. At that time the pessimists were afraid of two things: first, that any change in the political-economic line would not be enough to get rid of the lawlessness of public life; second, that the reforms, even on a strictly material level, would be obstructed by the administrative machine, which remained unchanged. These fears found expression in a joke of the time: "Johnny, do you see those sparrows on the branch?" "Yes, Pete, I see they've come right back, but every one of them on another branch." "Ah, but of course, Johnny, that's what they call Renovation."

When I came back from Oslo and the customs inspector cut my soap in half, I must already have been suspect. Of what I did not know: perhaps of being a political courier for my daughter, who had taken part in the student strike. After a while I realized that I was suspect in a much wider sense. I belonged to the *suspect category*—people who were aware of the extent of the evil at the very heart of public life. They had raised our wages but not restored confidence in our rights; they had built housing blocks, but not recreated the psychological link between man and his work. I belong to the group of people suspected of wanting to inspect the workings of the system and discover its weaknesses. That is inexcusable, because—as I told you—the function of the system is to reproduce itself; its job is to maintain its illegalities. Since I was suspected of an urge to show the superiority of truth over error, they deprived me of my post as lecturer at the university, and after a month of Renovation—transferred me to an office in a silent building, far from my students. If you are interested in seeing into the mind and behavior of such a suspect and in gauging what threats surround him, I shall try to enlighten you—not for my own satisfaction, but because it will help me to fill out what I have touched on in answering certain questions in the survey.

While I do that, I shall return to question twenty-five: *Is criticism of the government and of public institutions possible in your country? In what way may it be expressed? In what position does it place the person who criticizes?*

In Poland, the right to criticize the government is included in the Constitution. But in practice, any impulse of this kind can result in losing one's job or in harassment. Criticism therefore remains unspoken or is disguised. In general, it is expressed by a certain manner of living which I described as a refusal to remain merely functional. And I will say it again, the person who decides to follow such a course becomes suspect in the eyes of power. He must therefore take the consequences of his decision. These can be many, good and bad. He feels unwelcome among the mass—a mass which seem to him increasingly stupefied and dull; but as he appears among them precisely as a suspect, that very fact makes him stand out from the uniform dullness. Being suspected of thinking for himself, the suspicion comforts his inner self, gives him the feeling of living in a way that is both worthy of remark and personal to him. One could almost say that to be suspect does him good, that he finds in it a kind of grace. It is because he is separated from the mass that he begins to dwell in a reality richer in meaning, devoid of ready-made responses such as is manufactured for the mass; a reality which has, instead of answers, questions: the important questions, the eternal ones about such things as liberty, truth, God, and death. Such a life is less organized than the sphere of political intrigue; one has less right to protection than when one belongs to the "nomenclature." Yet, the experiences one finds in it are more interesting, even though they go with certain kinds of danger, to which I will return.

I should like at this point to inject a word of caution. From what I have just said you could get the impression that in my view the suspected person retreats into his shell and is isolated from the outside world. That is not at all my notion. In my view, he has a much clearer and more truthful perception of the outside world than the person poisoned by television and the press. He reads with greater insight and listens more acutely. The key that has been given him enables him to decipher the government's language. He answers suspicion with suspicion. To protect himself against made-up truths or half-truths, he doesn't need to go in search of the philosopher's stone; he looks for fuller information. He seeks out other sources—and these are always available—and that is how he eludes the grip of the official story. All this is within reach of everyone; only, you see, not everyone wants to take the consequences; only a few want to think. If you ask me what such a man thinks, well, a man under a cloud begins to see more clearly. Provided he is endowed with a good memory, and is well-informed and does not give in to the propaganda machine or allow the system to reduce him to silence, he sees a world of constant threats. He expects every minute that somewhere in the world something is going on counter to reason. He expects that nobody can fight the regime when it scorns the law and declares there is a worldwide plot fomented by—let me see—all the redheads. He expects that when people hear this accusation on the news, even if they don't believe it, they will get the idea just the same that it is not a good idea to defend redheads.

Such a man feels he is the object of ever-increasing suspicion, while to him it is the world that becomes more and more suspect. So here we are again: such a lucid and clean-cut perception of reality inevitably leads him to the point where he must reorganize this reality within himself. Otherwise life becomes unbearable. Anyhow, he cannot help asking himself several elementary questions. I tried to answer them myself in addressing myself to yours. Now I should like to talk about the worst of the dangers that I mentioned to you: the danger of becoming once more naive.

I don't know if you realize what it means to think in a society that has long since lost the habit. In this connection, conspiring has not proved to be the best of schools. In the years after the underground, a person who wanted to think had first to plan how he could ensure his own protection. He would exhaust himself in trying to stand upright after his dialectical somersaults and struggles with ideology. That was the era of chaos and weariness. Everywhere, there was nothing but bankruptcy and ideological revisionism. The West had nothing to offer except its slogan about the end of ideology and a literature of despair or the absurd. In a cabaret, some students put on a show with the ironic title of *Thinking Has a Colossal Future*, and a few French plays were also being performed in which the characters expressed themselves in gastric rumblings. A few years later, our man (the suspect) noticed that he was living in a world whose language had become incomprehensible to him. He would sit in front of his television to watch, stupefied, the pictures come and go. What—just then—was he thinking about? About the very things which used to torture him as a schoolboy writing his diary. What is man? Does God exist? Does death mean the end, and how ought one to live? These are actually an adolescent's questions; if you ask them, the fear of being laughed at is well justified. Dare we ask them in a civilization where research by specialists has replaced philosophy? Our world, which is interested in technology, in genetics, and in the structure of language, has grown humble in the face of the universal

157

problems; it has set itself narrower, better defined goals. In such a world, to go deep within oneself and ponder the secrets of Being, without electronic microscopes, without laboratories or accelerators—that can only be the quirk of a thinker from the provinces seeking a proof of the existence of God. Yet sometimes there is nothing else to do. When choosing a way of life, only naive questions remain, because in such a world all questions with an ethical content appear to be naive.

Be that as it may, the man suspected of wanting to think has more leisure to ask such questions. In a sense, it is his thirteenth month's pay. And everything depends on the way he is going to spend it. In general, those who have been disappointed by the outcome of revolutionary utopias run the risk of making a hundred-and-eighty-degree turn; that is, of rejecting everything implied by revolution. But to reject revolution as too brutal a method of changing social life is not without consequences. I know intelligent and honorable people who moved away from Marxism, or from having an interest in Marxism, to opinions belonging to the traditional, conservative right. They were swept into it by one crisis, one shock after another; they tore off their old skin and ended up no longer able to understand the present-day world. The revolutionary movements in Asia and Latin America, as well as the tendencies of the new left in Western Europe, all of that is something inconceivable to them, suicidal. To them revolution heralds the slavery that is to come. They are beyond understanding that in certain situations revolution can get rid of obstacles to development and become one of the moral forces, while at other times it is up to the moral forces themselves to repair the damage caused by revolution. And there, too, lies another danger: that those who manage to escape one set of ready-made

158

ideas can be engulfed by another set diametrically opposite. Alas! So it goes—which is not to say that it is inevitable. In short, let us say that he who goes in for thinking for himself travels a road full of pitfalls.

There is yet another danger. The fundamental principle of the system is the solidarity of the entire nation in the establishment of socialism. Everybody works; education, art, and culture are for everybody, apartments and televisions likewise. No distinction is made between the working class and the creative intelligentsia—all share the same goal and work for a people's Poland. Yet, not everybody wants the same things and people are not all identical. Some work better than others, some like this socialism, others think that true socialism would be the exact opposite. Some have a leftist view of the world, others lean toward fascism; there are many practicing Catholics and many who are indifferent to religion. In addition, there are cynics and careerists who don't give a damn about anything. There are also those who desire real betterment. In a word, there are social traditions which can be said to perpetuate the characteristic features and the social forces of prewar Poland. One can still recognize the attitudes and ways of thought of, for example, the Christian Democrats or the Social Democrats, the Communists or the conservatives, and one can determine roughly who, before the war, sympathized with the peasant left or with the extreme right, and who was liable to collaborate with any regime whatever. But all this goes on under a bushel; it is compressed and leveled by the steamroller of the system. Everything is flattened, reduced to one dimension; no individual opinions may be heard, there is but one political program. Some turn out to be in accord with this state of affairs, others take part in it openly, with more or less enthusiasm. But there are others

159

still, those I am talking about here, who cannot accept it, who do not want it. This does not mean that they share a common point of view or have similar preferences. No, they differ. But they find themselves in the position of suspects who, rather than devour one another, must emphasize what unites them. In practice, that tends to minimize differences and bring about false alliances. I see in that yet another threat of nongenuineness. Suppressing differences leads to stifling contradictions artificially, which in turn blunts the sharpness of thought. Those who have escaped the trap of the system shackle themselves within a new trap, where they may also come to be stifled. The conservative will suffocate beside the liberal, the Catholic beside the socialist: they fail to expose their ideological conflicts in the light of day, they bathe in forced solidarity, create the semblance of mutual agreement, and condemn any of their number who try to avoid pretense. It is only one step from this to accusations of treason and provocation. And even if this step is not taken, there is always the risk that one will mute one's own truths and principles, and give up fighting, which is a natural urge, for the triumph of one's ideas. Such is the price we pay for the lack of a public life; culture pays it with psychic maladies and with a certain lag in general intelligence. How can one overcome this? I have no answer—which does not mean that no answer exists.

The fourth danger that a person who disassociates himself from the mass must confront is that he will become suspect to it. He will be suspect in the eyes of the mass because the mass wants to have food, clothing, and an automobile, to be entertained with films and songs. The average prefer good eating and entertainment to thought. Thought represents an effort; it means anxiety and risk. The mass is made up of millions whose heritage is the memory of poverty, war, and fear. The present level of development—the satisfaction of material and cultural needs, the feeling of physical security—has bred in them an entirely new sense of property. This is an acquisition definitely theirs and which they do not want to lose. So they are afraid to express doubts or to ask questions that would jeopardize their newly won status as owners. The mass, today, does not like abstract ideas. When one speaks of freedom or justice, they only listen with reluctance. Those are threatening words, they interrupt the humdrum of daily life, and the consequences they entail are unforeseeable. Nor do the masses like to hear talk about moral courage, because they see it as an expense beyond their means and which could ruin them. He who thinks independently of the mass should remember this; it is the most painful danger he can expect to risk. It is a professional risk, a risk associated with his calling. The people have turned to stone not only the witches, but also the philosophers, the teachers, and the doctors.

That's that: what next? You notice that I've avoided saying "the intelligentsia," because, as I've already mentioned, I am not sure of its present meaning. Yet all the while I have in mind a certain type of man whom one formerly regarded as belonging to the intelligentsia. Today they are given to understand that their role is over. They are told, more or less to their face, you have ceased to be the conscious part of the nation; be satisfied with exercising your profession and obeying. The intelligentsia is allowed to work at making discoveries, but within the confines of specialties. To reinstate the historical tradition of that sociocultural class would be an anachronism: problems and scruples, opposition and protest—all that, for the machinery of power, is nothing more than kindergarten play. I am not the originator of that expression; it has been used of those who have the time to think as individuals. Yet in spite of everything such people exist and multiply. It is what is called today the reproduction of the elite and what it means in fact is the birth among the younger generations of a type of man who is against mass existence and who thinks for himself. The existence and the rebirth of this type of individual is certainly the most unexpected of Polish miracles.

I may be telling you about my own situation here, but you must not think it applies only to an isolated case; it applies rather to a small number of men who are more perceptive than others. I said that I did not feel I had the strength to set out guidelines and even less to propose a plan of action. I am barely able to anticipate the future, to express theories, wishes, hopes. That's all and it isn't much.

One of the questions in the survey has to do with [my] *idea of the role of the family in the present-day world*. I don't know what to tell you. In my view, the family in its traditional meaning of a social unit has ceased to exist both economically and morally. But I wouldn't undertake to prove it. I am close to my daughter by virtue of our good understanding and the apartment we share. But we eat separately and our ideas, similar on some subjects, differ on others. I shall not be leaving her a legacy. From time to time we lend each other modest sums of money. But I honestly do not know whether we constitute a social unit, and if so, I do not know its function. Nevertheless, I am sure that nonnatural families, those based on spiritual bonds, could play a very important role today. I have in mind not those intellectual communities born of fashion and mass initiation, but those which challenge them. The moment when one passes from one grouping into another is sometimes very interesting. A young geologist and mountain climber told my daughter one day that after scaling a vertical rock face and while he was sitting ecstatic on a ledge, he suddenly realized that during the previous five years he had shown himself incapable of standing up to the secretary of the Party organization. He began to wonder if his love of mountain climbing did not conceal a wish to replace integrity with dangerous feats. He said he felt like an eagle in the mountains but like a dishrag down below. He had, without knowing, come up against theology's dilemma: is there or isn't there a clash in man between nature created and nature increate, between body and soul? After his return from the climb, he was thrown out of the party for having stated formally that socialism could not be constructed by leveling down. The young man no longer lives in flat country. He is working right now as a guide in the Tatras and may be said to enjoy the status of suspect element.

It seems to me that only people who are suspect, and suspect for this kind of reason, can become the source of nonmaterial values in a system where no signpost points upward. Such people constitute an unexploited but productive capital. They form a reserve for the dark days. The personality of a nation does not depend on statistics that are rousing, but primarily on goals that rouse men. At times when optimism is strong in me, I think about those "elective affinities," those imponderables, and the merits of a humanistic universe, all of which bring up historical analogies. For example, did not Freemasonry constitute a deliberate effort to oppose Puritanism and the Counter-Reformation, an attempt to find a common ground outside the system? Did not the earliest Christian communities struggle against the bureaucratic and materialistic structure of the Roman Empire? You may say that Christianity came from below, whereas the King of

Prussia was a mason. True, but the Holy Cross found its way into Caesar's chambers and the Masonic lodges helped to build the Western democracies. Both of the "common grounds," despite their differences, turned out to have a future which it would have been difficult to foresee.

But it takes work. Culture takes work—a collective effort, an exchange of ideas, the assembling of many documents and pieces of testimony. People must correspond with one another, they must write polemics, memoirs, and reports, and not just works of fiction. The people of the eighteenth and nineteenth centuries had the habit of such activities; they were not lazy when it came to recording events and expressing ideas. Their minds were rigorous even in conversation; they used to *construct* their conversations! With us, private conversation is generally superficial and anecdotal, and taped discussions, intended for publication, are never totally candid. Letters? Reports? Public statements? Private diaries? They are all inhibited, either because they are submitted to an internal censorship or because they are produced on demand. There can be no social consciousness unless the communication between minds is continual. And such communication requires an active, enduring, and genuine access to the world of culture. Social consciousness needs a workshop; we must be craftsmen building what is to survive us. If not, fifty years from now, those who resemble us will all be slaves. Perhaps they will feel better inside than we do; perhaps they will be happier than we are—they will then be willing slaves.

When I speak of a community of suspects and their solidarity, I am in no way forgetting the problems they face. But I consider that their task is a feasible one, if only in the *way* that they communicate. In conversation, for example, for language can also be a form of freedom. Men who are capable of expressing their thoughts and their feelings in a language of their own, men who are masters of their ideas and the meaning of their words, such men escape the consensus. To make use of a strictly personal idiom in describing events is to take a step toward liberty, and it is a step that can be taken at any time, anywhere. And here we must begin, because it is feasible. If you remember, I have already given my views on *the principal dangers that threaten contemporary man*. I linked this part of the questionnaire with my answer to another question and in so doing skipped the following one: *What* [in my view] *are the most important needs of contemporary man?*

Answer: needs that do not yet exist. Needs of which the majority of people are not aware. There was a time when they were called dreams, ideals. Today those words are not used. But my father used them. He got them from the last century and wanted to leave me their common denominator: *independence*. But I grew up in the twentieth century in a free country which did not know how to solve its real problems. To me, independence meant thirty million men with unequal incomes, exposed to unemployment and to the police and their bludgeons. To him, it remained forever an idea synonymous with liberty. When he died, in September 1944, he was evacuating a casualty of the Uprising. This first-aid officer was sixty years old. I like to think he was among those happy and courageous men who have lived and died in peace; who, after the First World War, helped organize systems of education, health, and justice; who, during the Second, took part in the fight against the occupation forces and gave underground training. They did not have to do research and invent anything. Their conception of the world was waiting for them at birth; they came into the world as heirs to destiny—with principles, allegories, and a calendar of heroes descended straight from the world of their fathers. As for me, I could not make myself their heir without a few objections. I scented something like the odor of incense, an absurd and courtly hypocrisy, a gentleman's fear when confronted by the nakedness of facts, and I also detected a kind of cowardice. Perhaps I had the right to think that way during an era that has been called "the contemptuous years." But then what's the right name for the present era? The new powers have turned my father's spiritual world into television cartoons. I see the nation embattled, yes, but at the same time I understand how much of it all is a technical trick. For the purpose of the program is to hold the spectator's attention on the past, to draw it away from the present-day need to battle and toward some imaginary event. One can make out the spots where the film has been touched up— the picture has been redrawn so that it fulfills its role of "diversion" while preserving the semblance of truth. Granted, the image my father had of the world was an illusion, but it gave him an ideal of liberty. The pictures one sees today merely perpetuate an inner slavery. And make no mistake, the power machine knows fully as much as I what freedom is and what slavery is, and it does an admirable job of managing the game of appearances. It understands perfectly well that falsifying liberty is the best way to perpetuate slavery. The machine is fully conscious. It knows that one can exhibit the nation on the screen with as little risk as an abstract painting in a museum. A film then creates the illusion of a full life—tradition *plus* modernity, every spiritual need satisfied. All except one. Nothing makes the machine tremble more than the thought of a good understanding among men, of their realization in common that their rights have been flouted and ignored. The nation's freedom—and this also the machine knows—is conditional upon the rights of individuals. And that is what the machine is afraid of: that when the people find each other and recognize each other in the darkness, all of a sudden the lights might go on and somebody might have to turn off the projector. Amen.

I repeat: that is the optimism in me speaking, those are my hopes. And what if they do not materialize? Well then, we shall see . . . Icz's most recent prophecy coming to pass. I ran into him shortly before I left Warsaw, in front of the International Bookstore. In a low voice and with a knowing air, he told me that within the next two generations Poland would die a civil death, a spiritual smothering, after which it would be eaten up by the technocracy of the two worlds. And in a still lower voice, with a still more knowing air, he added: "Unless a new consciousness appears and prevents it all . . ." Then he went toward the bookstore to buy the latest publication of the Catholic Press. One must always take seriously the predictions of Icz.

Enough for today. Tomorrow I am to meet the unknown gentleman and I will have to inform him that behind the "Rondo" cell there was—nothing. I don't know who he is or what he wants. I expect an unpleasant interview. What's more, I am not prepared. Why did I ever get the idea of creating something which did not exist? If I tell him that it was for love of a woman he will not believe me and he will be right. I had other motives. I've already spoken of the great cost of conspiracy, the garbled and unnatural ideas they produce. In every form of social life there is a kind of necessary evil which is not overcome by myths and legends until later. In "Rondo" I wanted to get over that necessary evil immediately, produce the myth in its pure form, and not pay for the legend. For in the end, what is the best product of experience if it is not the best lie with which to envelop it? I wanted the converse—to make the best experience out of the lie. Still, I have lingering doubts as to the validity of my reasoning.

Chapter 11

EIGHT O'CLOCK. Do you hear a drumming noise on the tape? That's the sound of rain. Here in the room it's getting darker and darker; outside it hasn't stopped pouring. A minute ago I opened the window on the balcony and the smell of rotting fish invaded my room. I am sitting down. I do not have to speed to the airport on the wet highway and that is enough for me. I feel well. I am trying to speak a little louder because the tape must certainly be picking up the hammering of the rain.

He turned out to be the son of the prompter in *The Wedding*; I knew his mother. I remember that when I was working as an extra she brought me a piece of bread and cheese during the intermission, with an apple and a copy of the Old Testament. She liked to see me eat and to talk to me about the end of the world—the earth drowning in blood: she was a Jehovah's Witness. Later, during the first few months of the war, in winter, I worked in the cloakroom of the actors' café, and she, Madame Lala, was the cashier. Her son found something better; he is sales representative for an American electronics firm, West Electric, if I heard right. He told me that his mother died just after the war, in the town of Z . . . where he was born.

I remembered him after I had a drink. At first I thought there was some mistake or that it was a practical joke. The bewhiskered face meant nothing to me; it looked like the faces of millions of travelers seen in international airports or tourist buses. Smoking a pipe gave me leave to be silent; I had decided not to make conversation but just to wait. And I was waiting for the earliest opportunity to make my excuses and get away. But when he began to tell me how he had brought a soaking-wet suitcase from the East End Station and then smiled: "You let me stay overnight because it was after the curfew . . . ," suddenly, I saw him again, standing in the middle of my room, with his cardboard suitcase, his overcoat, and his old shoes full of water. I knew him: Anek, the only son of Madame Lala. It was at his mother's request that I recommended him to my father, who had begun to teach underground classes in Zoliborz. I knew that his mother was afraid for him, and it was after a conversation in which she had told me that two of his classmates had been arrested that I decided to have him join "Rondo." At that time I needed to enroll some new couriers.

I did not immediately understand how I could help him now. His flight for Tokyo did not leave for another two hours. Business with the Japanese, he said. I noticed that he kept looking at his watch. Good, I thought to myself, this time you're going to do something else in the plane than study your files. I'm going to give you a different sort of food for thought. But I felt myself warming to him precisely because he did not say anything. He did talk about his mother, and at one point I wondered if he had wanted to see me just in order to talk about her. He said she had been very fond of me. I interrupted to ask when he had left Poland. He had fled across Germany at the time of the first arrests, then had settled in Canada. He felt he had burnt his bridges behind him; moreover, the news of my arrest had come to him in

Germany. He thought me long since dead. Do you know what he said? He said he had dreamed about me for years, several at least. He was caught, arrested with the suitcase, and forced to confess that it was I who had ordered him to deliver the encoded messages. He even pointed to me with his finger in his dream. Happening to turn on his television a few days earlier, he had been shocked to see me, so much so that for a minute he thought I was addressing him from beyond the grave.

It is our old friend again, the betrayal complex. Yet I must say that for a Lord Jim he was not devoid of tact. Clearly he was not going to wallow in sentimentality. He spoke tersely, at times almost drily. As for me, I did not like it at all. I had stopped drinking and I felt more and more unwell. The whole thing was obvious to the point of stupidity and yet impossible to explain. To make him understand a "fiction" dating back thirty years, to rehearse my reasons, enumerate in detail circumstances that the passage of time had buried deep—it all seemed senseless. And apart from that I could foresee his reaction: he would be convinced that I was trying to cover my tracks. If I told him I had not been arrested he would wonder what means had been used to obtain my silence. I knew his type of man—blessed with an altogether clear and calculating mind. After all, when one sells for an electronics firm, one must possess a certain psychology. He had certainly read Conrad during the occupation, and now he wanted to remember his romantic youth. But I had no wish to remain in his memory as the captain of an abandoned ship. I was determined to explain everything; I was only putting off the moment. I wanted to do it as quickly and as late as possible. So when he looked at his watch again and asked if he could drive me back, I accepted. My hotel is on the way to the airport. At the bar he paid the bill with a little blue card and he blushed when he saw I was watching him. As he got behind the wheel he made it clear that it was a rented car and that the agency would pick it up at the airport parking lot. He evidently wanted to minimize his standard of living for my benefit. It was disarming, but at the same time I wanted to laugh as if somebody was tickling me. Who had thought up the tale anyway?—a wet suitcase filled with detective stories . . . the East End Station . . . "Rondo" . . . Tokyo . . . West Electric. In front of the hotel, without taking his hands off the steering wheel, he said to me, "Excuse me for taking up your time." And I replied, laughing, "It seems to me there was a time when I took up yours." And I could not say another word. I did not get out of the car. My mind was a blank, as used to happen at school, at the blackboard, when fear would make me forget a lesson I knew by heart. We both smiled without exactly looking at each other, and suddenly I suggested that I go to the airport with him. He turned to me and something must have snapped inside him. He said: "Yes, yes of course!" I heard the squeal of the tires on the pavement and for a moment I was petrified. I cursed my stupid idea; we were already on the highway and just then, the rain began to batter the windshield. It was as if he had gone mad. He was driving on the wet road at 200 k.p.h. and telling me about the best days of his life, drowning the sound of the rain with his shouting. The best days of his life—when he carried coded messages in a suitcase, when a girl in the train had slept with her head on his shoulder. . . . And now, I thought, we are about to die, we are going to get killed on this road, and it may not be the worst end for us. At the same time I felt curious; I could not understand what he was trying to say. He was talking about the girl in the train and I could have sworn he said, "She couldn't come with me, but I have told her a great deal about you." No, wait a minute, I must have misunderstood: *who* couldn't come? And I had a moment's panic. Without slowing down, this madman was driving with his left hand and searching for something in his pocket with his right. His wallet, he had brought out his wallet!

I gave him back the photographs at the very last minute; he was being paged on the loudspeaker. I remember that in one of them a young woman held two little boys in her arms. The other was no doubt taken at a later date: the same young woman was reading a book on a sofa with colorful cushions. He had met her on the train when he was bringing back a cardboard suitcase from Siedlce. She had gone to sleep on his shoulder, he had woken her when they reached Warsaw, they got off the train together, and then she confessed that she was Jewish and had nowhere to spend the night. She had fled during a raid, she was exhausted and hungry. From the station he had taken her to his mother's house, which he left to meet me with his soaked suitcase, just before the curfew. "She lived with my mother until the Uprising, and we were married in Montreal as soon as she could join me there."

I bought a bottle of bourbon in the airport bar and then got on a bus which was taking in some Air France passengers. I was lucky to get back and I'm in a fairly good mood. If somebody asked me "Are you all right?" I would say, "Okay." It seems that's the way my daughter's friends answer such questions. There are several reasons for my good humor. Outside the window I can see the convention delegates who are now getting out of three huge buses which have stopped right in front of the hotel. They are returning from an excursion of a couple of days, and over the sound of the rain one can make out the voices and shouts of theaterologists from the five continents. If I hadn't declined to join this excursion, I would now be leaping over puddles to hear the news that a certain Mr. -ski had sent me greetings over the telephone before leaving for Tokyo. It is hot, and from time to time I think back to "Rondo" and its offspring. Because those two children laughing in the photograph are after all the children of "Rondo" and thus, in a way, my daughter's brothers. It is strange, but I feel like the father of a species, like a symbolic father who must have kept the secret of the Creation to himself. Love, lies, chance, error, and blood have contributed to my fiction, making it into a creation of life. Everything has gone on in accordance with the order of things to perpetuate love, to repeat mistakes, to let us be trifled with by chance and by fiction, and to shed blood. But it was a good job, no one has done anything better and I really have no reason today to feel unhappy.

Ten thirty. I'm sure all over again that it would have been better to stick to the questions in their due order. I did not adhere to any rules, I spoke in a disorganized fashion, choosing my subjects as I liked and allowing myself to digress. What this has yielded I don't know—perhaps the rough outline of an autobiography or a sort of internal portrait. But it seems to me that even looking at it that way I haven't achieved my purpose. Never mind. In any case, my tapes communicate, they make up a certain number of hours of text, which must mean something or at least are of some psychological or sociological interest. Of course, knowing that I shall become a subject for analysis fills me with dread. I said so at the beginning and now I feel it even more keenly and I think it a good idea to forestall it.

First, my answers can be discredited on an intellectual level. To an intellectual of today they will seem like an unbelievable anachronism, almost infantile, especially when I touch on subjects which have been debated over

174

and over by classical philosophy and moral science. I am aware of this; I have called it "a return to the beginning." I see in this return to the fundamental distinction between Good and Evil the possibility of escaping from a world that has become stereotyped by the ideas fed to the masses. For I do think that the phenomena of mass society constitute the latest form of oppression, and that one cannot resist them with anything except the moral will of the individual. I mean the will in its most elemental form, controlled by the simplest and most ancient commandments: first, blind-and-deaf resistance, and then argument. I foresee your objections and stop there.

I expect that the young sociologists who will work on my answers will be shocked by a number of complexes which they will find incomprehensible. They will come upon names, dates, and places which will mean nothing to them. Assure them that these are local problems, Polish problems. Your collaborators will no doubt be surprised to see to what extent these local problems influence my relation to contemporary life. I accept the criticism, but on one condition. In being aware that I lag behind modern Western thought, and realizing that my brain is encumbered with Polish complexes, I am also and equally aware of the reasons for this state of fact. I live in a country which for two hundred years has been compelled to adopt the reflex of self-defense, in a country which has only survived by means of prayers, of secret universities, and of banned books; a country which, at a time when Western societies were achieving unity, had only one goal, to survive. It has been called a feud among neighbors. An outstanding French thinker put the same thing in stronger words: "The Poles are all bedeviled by the bloody Russians!" What he meant was that our obsession with the Russians lies heavy on our consciousness and that we owe our peculiar mentality to our monster of a neighbor. But his typically French way of expressing himself is too epigrammatic to be accurate. It requires at least a few more words of explanation and a few historical reminders, including some about the history of France.

I imagine also that I could be accused of being anachronistic in insisting so much on the importance of rights. It seems out of place to people who enjoy multiple rights, but please try to understand what I am talking about. I am speaking of another world, another education. Life has a natural tendency to produce false, illusory images. Life overrides our knowledge, we are puppets before its climaxes and forgeries. We get lost amid its chaos and so we try to organize it by relying upon rights. Polish life has for a long time raised this attempt to the highest degree. It has given birth to the greatest number of monsters and illusions, these glorifications and these communal devotions that have not been measured with reference to rights. Indeed, the opposite has been true. They have been substituted for rights; rights have been made out of them. The lack of a state of its own has brought about in Poland a peculiar situation: the surrender of real to imaginary power. It is the political acting out of this situation that we are witnessing today. That is why I talk about rights. I talk about them because they alone will enable us to leave this magic-lantern show, which offers society a semblance of freedom instead of freedom, and folk costumes instead of a public life. I talk about rights, because they alone permit the ordering and organization of the individual, of society, and of humanity whose joint harmony has been destroyed in Poland by the glorification of the nation. But the nation also consists of rights. One might repeat here Mickiewicz's opinion as reported by one of his most believable interviewers: "The Turks are in general more honest than the French, but the French form a better society than the Turks because they have better laws." It is after 1848 that he is said to have uttered those words.

I have also talked about rights because the majority of people in Poland do not realize to what extent they need them. I do not know if a people anywhere else right now, any other society, is as starved for rights.

All this should do by way of answer for a study with a sociological base, for a survey. But wait—you will say to yourself—these are a man's confidential thoughts about his life and about ideas, neither of which are representative of his society. I willingly accept this criticism, but only on certain terms. I am *not* an exception: many people in Poland live and think like me. My life is one version among others of the experiences of my generation, and plenty of people share the opinions that I profess here. Everything I have said in my own name could have been said in the third person without sounding improbable. But I am afraid that even then it would be impossible to avoid the tone of the confessional.

You have difficulty understanding this in your part of the world, but with us, the human situations are more drastic.

Chapter 12

THE FINAL TAPE. I looked at the questionnaire again to make sure that I hadn't overlooked anything on it. I see I have skipped only four questions.

Do you often resort to the help of a psychiatrist?

Do you concede the possibility that our planet could be extinguished? Does thinking about this make you depressed?

What is your view of the institution of marriage in today's world? Do you accept marriages between homosexuals?

If you could be born again, and choose the place and date of your birth, what sort of choice would you make?

I can't tell you why I skipped those questions. But I will leave them unanswered and would ask you to attribute their omission to fatigue.

I have been working for several days at Studio XX. I'm aware that I haven't told you anything about the play I am directing. It is a play in two acts, composed according to the poetics of the ballads of the Middle Ages. I say "according to the poetics" because it is evident that the work is an intentional stylization, and a remarkable one, indeed. It must have been written much later, probably at the beginning of the nineteenth century. It is about a young Irish girl seduced by a lord. Actually, the lord does not realize that it is he who has been seduced by the girl. There are five parts in the cast and I hope to have the opening four weeks hence. Uth Seenzen plays the part of the seductress.

So much for that—and I think that is all.

At Studio XX they will make a copy of these tapes for me. I should like to keep them for myself, I will take them back to Warsaw. They do not contain anything that goes against the Constitution; in fact, the Constitution gives me permission to bring them in. Anyhow, they can't be put into a cake of soap. I'll put them in the pocket of my coat.

Tomorrow I will return the tape recorder. All my thanks.